A Survey of Digital Humanities Centers in the United States

by Diane M. Zorich

November 2008

Council on Library and Information Resources

Washington, D.C.

ISBN 978-1-932326-31-4
CLIR Publication No. 143
Published by:

Council on Library and Information Resources
1752 N Street NW, Suite 800
Washington, DC 20036
Web site at http://www.clir.org

Additional copies are available for $25 each. Orders must be placed through CLIR's Web site.
This publication is also available online at no charge at http://www.clir.org/pubs/abstract/pub143abst.html.

 The paper in this publication meets the minimum requirements of the American National Standard for Information Sciences—Permanence of Paper for Printed Library Materials ANSI Z39.48-1984.

Cover image: © 2008 Cathy Gendron c/o theispot.com

Library of Congress Cataloging-in-Publication Data

Zorich, Diane.
 A survey of digital humanities centers in the United States / by Diane M. Zorich.
   p. cm.
 Includes bibliographical references.
 ISBN 978-1-932326-31-4 (alk. paper)
 1. Digital humanities centers--United States. 2. Humanities--Study and teaching--United States. 3. Humanities--United States--Information services. 4. Humanities--Research--United States. I. Title.

 AZ183.U5Z67 2008
 001.3071'073--dc22

                    2008045242

Contents

About the Author

Diane M. Zorich is a cultural heritage consultant specializing in planning and managing the delivery of cultural information. Her clients include the J. Paul Getty Trust, the American Association of Museums, the Smithsonian Institution, RLG Programs/OCLC, and many other cultural organizations and institutions.

Before establishing her consultancy, Ms. Zorich was data manager at the Association of Systematics Collections in Washington, D.C., and documentation manager at the Peabody Museum of Archaeology and Ethnology at Harvard University. She served as past president and Board member of the Museum Computer Network, and was chair of that organization's Intellectual Property Special Interest Group. She also served as project manager for *A Museum Guide to Copyright and Trademark* (American Association of Museums 1999) and *Cataloging Cultural Objects: A Guide to Describing Cultural Works and Their Images* (American Library Association 2007).

Ms. Zorich is the author of *Introduction to Managing Digital Assets: Options for Cultural and Educational Organizations* (The J. Paul Getty Trust 1999), *Developing Intellectual Property Policies: A "How-To" Guide for Museums* (Canadian Heritage Information Network 2003), and *A Survey of Digital Cultural Heritage Initiatives and Their Sustainability Concerns* (Council on Library and Information Resources 2003). She also co-authored *Beyond the Silos of the LAMs: Collaboration Among Libraries, Archives and Museums* (OCLC Programs and Research 2008) and her latest publication on information policies in museums appears in *Museum Informatics* (Routledge 2008).

Ms. Zorich has graduate degrees in anthropology and museum studies, and is based in Princeton, New Jersey.

Acknowledgments

The author thanks the leaders of the digital humanities centers who generously made time in their schedules to speak about their centers. I hope the findings presented in this report dispel any initial reactions they may have had to "yet another survey."

I also thank Lilly Nguyen and Katie Shilton of the Department of Information Studies at the University of California, Los Angeles, for agreeing to undertake the tool-accessibility study that accompanies this report, and for doing so in such an enthusiastic and methodical manner. My sincerest thanks to Dr. Amy Friedlander and Dr. Charles Henry of the Council on Library and Information Resources for the opportunity to undertake this project and for the guidance and insights they offered throughout the process.

During the period in which this survey was conducted, the directors of two of the digital humanities centers who participated in this study passed away. The legacy of Roy Rosenzweig (Center for History and New Media at George Mason University) and Ross Scaife (Collaboratory for Research in Computing for the Humanities at the University of Kentucky) continues through their centers.

Foreword

An unspoken question runs through Diane Zorich's detailed survey and analysis of digital humanities centers in the United States: Why do we need these centers, and what needs do they meet that traditional academic departments do not? The answer lies in her definition of a center, which she forged from a careful study of the ways in which centers themselves describe their missions, functions, and activities. Digital humanities centers, she writes, are entities "where new media and technologies are used for humanities-based research, teaching, and intellectual engagement and experimentation. The goals of the center are to further humanities scholarship, create new forms of knowledge, and explore technology's impact on humanities-based disciplines" (p. 4). In an environment where scholars identify with their disciplines rather than with their departments, and where significant professional affiliations or communities of interest may transcend the boundaries of scholars' colleges and universities, centers offer interdisciplinary "third places"—a term sociologist Ray Oldenburg has used to identify a social space, distinct from home and workplace. Third places foster important ties and are critical to community life. Familiar examples are barbershops, beauty salons, and coffee shops where, in the age of wireless, we see tables of students hunched over laptops, textbooks, and notepads. The academic library plays a role similar to that of a third place, providing resources, seminar rooms, and collaborative work spaces. It probably should not surprise us that both centers and libraries are frequently cited as elements in the emerging cyberinfrastructure to support advanced research in the sciences, technology, and humanities.

Zorich developed her definition by looking at the functions advertised by existing centers, that is, functions that centers claimed, rather than functions that might be ascribed to them. These functions range from building shared collections and tools to providing shared services, such as preservation, training, and lectures, to supporting faculty and students, among others. While any one of these functions might be available elsewhere, the center is distinguished by a critical mass of some subset of these functions, together with the ability to attract scholars with similar, interdisciplinary interests but different formal education and training and a shared commitment to using technology to further these interests. The technology is simultaneously a driver and an opportunity, and the centers, whether virtual or physical, effectively become safe places, hospitable to innovation and experimentation, as well as anchors from which to base the intellectual analog of civil society in which third places are vital parts.

Many of today's digital humanities centers are highly successful. They have incubated important research, fostered a generation of humanities scholars who are comfortable with the technology, devised creative modes of governance, assembled diverse portfolios of funding strategies, and built significant digital collections and suites of tools (the latter is the subject of Appendix F to this report by Lilly Nguyen and Katherine Shilton, graduate students at the University of California, Los Angeles). But the centers are also vulnerable. Funding can be precarious; talent is hired away, and since most of these centers are focused on their home institutions, they are at risk of becoming silos. Such institutional parochialism can inhibit the building of shared resources, like repositories, or of services, like long-term preservation, that represent a shared infrastructure where the impact of the shared resource is enhanced precisely because multiple parties contribute to and use it.

At the same time, building such infrastructure has advantages. It reduces costs to any one participant, minimizes unnecessary redundancy, and enables scholars to expand their thinking and research to take advantage of scale at precisely the moment when large-scale collections are becoming more likely as a result of mass-digitization projects or the proliferation of new media forms, particularly video, visualizations, scenarios, and simulations, which are data and computationally intensive. Increasingly, scholars seek ways to merge data from highly heterogeneous sources—text, audio, visual, multilingual, statistical, and so on—and to experiment with the material using new frameworks such as geographic information systems and social networks.

Shared infrastructure is not without perils, notably the free rider and moral hazard problems. The former occurs when one member of a network takes disproportionate advantage of the shared resource in excess of its contribution to it, and the latter when a member of a network takes risks that jeopardize the collective health and stability of the system. Individual institutions are understandably reluctant to become exposed to either scenario or to relinquish their identities, which may be bound up in collections, human talent, and facilities that have contributed to their success. Overcoming these barriers requires compromise, negotiation, and, ultimately, trust. Infrastructure systems are simultaneously technological, social, and organizational systems, and like all cooperative social systems, they rest on trust. That trust may be interpersonal, like the mutual trust between coauthors, or institutionalized, as made evident in shared practice, codes of conduct, and formal agreements. Such norms change as expectations evolve, which means that building infrastructure requires ongoing negotiation to ensure that the fundamental trust mechanisms that enable the infrastructure itself remain secure.

How we do that is a challenge, fraught with ambiguity as well as opportunity. To borrow a metaphor from William Shakespeare, whose hero in *Hamlet* was contemplating indecision and action, the future, like death, is an undiscovered country, "from whose bourn, No traveller returns." Experience can be a guide, however, and this report, grounded in experience and tempered by rigorous analysis, provides us footing as we move forward to build infrastructure to support a new generation of scholarship.

Amy Friedlander
Director of Programs

Executive Summary

In preparation for the 2008 Scholarly Communications Institute (SCI 6) focused on humanities research centers, the Council on Library and Information Resources (CLIR) commissioned a survey of digital humanities centers (DHCs). The immediate goals of the survey were to identify the extent of these centers and to explore their financing, organizational structure, products, services, and sustainability. The longer-term goal was to provide SCI 6 participants with a greater understanding of existing centers to inform their discussions about regional and national centers. The yearlong study took place in two phases: (1) a planning phase during which a working definition of DHC was developed, selection criteria were established, candidates were identified, and methodology was planned; and (2) an implementation phase during which the survey was conducted and responses analyzed. Thirty-two organizations took part in the survey, which was conducted through interviews with senior management, and through Web site and literature reviews of the participating DHCs.

The results show that DHCs can be grouped into two general categories:

1. Center focused: Centers organized around a physical location, with many diverse projects, programs, and activities undertaken by faculty, researchers, and students. These centers offer a wide array of resources to diverse audiences. Most DHCs operate under this model.

2. Resource focused: Centers organized around a primary resource, located in a virtual space, that serve a specific group of members. All programs and products flow from the resource, and individual and institutional members help sustain the resource by providing content, labor, or other support services.

The study findings also show that DHCs are entering a new phase of organizational maturity, with concomitant changes in activities, roles, and sustainability. Of late, there is a growing interest in fostering greater communication among centers to leverage their numbers for advocacy efforts. However, few DHCs have considered whether an unfettered proliferation of individual centers is an appropriate model for advancing humanities scholarship. Indeed, some features in the current landscape of centers may inadvertently hinder wider research and scholarship. These include the following:

1. The silo-like nature of current centers is creating untethered digital production that is detrimental to the needs of humanities

scholarship. Today's centers favor individual projects that address specialized research interests. These projects are rarely integrated into larger digital resources that would make them more widely known and available for the research community. As a result, they receive little exposure outside their center and are at greater risk of being orphaned over time.

2. The independent nature of existing centers does not effectively leverage resources community-wide. Centers have overlapping agendas and activities, particularly in training, digitization of collections, and metadata development. Redundant activities across centers are an inefficient use of the scarce resources available to the humanities community.

3. Large-scale, coordinated efforts to address the "big" issues in building a humanities cyberinfrastructure, such as repositories that enable long-term access to the centers' digital production, are missing from the current landscape. Collaborations among existing centers are small and focus on individual partner interests; they do not scale up to address community-wide needs.

The findings of this survey suggest that new models *are* needed for large-scale cyberinfrastructure projects, for cross-disciplinary research that cuts a wide swathe across the humanities, and for integrating the huge amounts of digital production already available. Current DHCs will continue to have an important role to play, but that role must be clarified in the context of the broader models that emerge.

When one is investigating collaborative models for humanities scholarship, the sciences offer a useful framework. Large-scale collaborations in the sciences have been the subject of research that examines the organizational structures and behaviors of these entities and identifies the criteria needed to ensure their success. The humanities should look to this work in planning its own strategies for regional or national models of collaboration.

1. Introduction: Survey Background and Goals

In preparation for the 2008 Scholarly Communications Institute (SCI 6) focused on humanities research centers, the Council on Library and Information Resources (CLIR) commissioned a survey of digital humanities centers (DHCs). The immediate goals of the survey were to identify the extent of these centers and to explore their financing, organizational structure, products, services, and sustainability. The longer-term goal was to provide SCI 6 participants with a greater understanding of existing centers to inform their discussions about regional and national centers.

The program description for SCI 6 notes:

> While it is necessary to more clearly define the notion and characteristics of such national centers, there is a danger in doing it too soon, in letting current and past models structure the future. . . . the discussion and options for centers [should remain] open until the scholarly community has had ample opportunity to identify and consider various models.

This CLIR survey contributes to the discussion by providing information on current DHC models, their benefits and limitations, and the range and reach of DHC activities. With this baseline information, SCI participants could consider whether current models are adequately addressing the changing nature of humanities scholarship or whether new models are needed.

The survey also explores the collaborative aspect of existing models. As digital humanities computing becomes an integrative, multiteam endeavor, the motivations, support structures, and reward systems that make for successful collaboration become critically important. Survey participants were asked about their experiences forming and sustaining partnerships, consortia, and other joint efforts to gauge the role of collaboration in the operations of these centers and to highlight aspects of collaboration that may be critical to the success of regional or national centers.

The yearlong study was conducted in two phases. During Phase I (June–August 2007), the planning stage, a working definition of a digital humanities center was developed and then used to identify and select survey participants. In addition, the survey questionnaire and methodology were devised. During Phase II (September 2007–May 2008), the survey was implemented and results were analyzed.

2. Selection of Survey Participants

2.1 Defining a Digital Humanities Center

Because digital humanities centers are self-defined entities that exhibit a variety of characteristics and conduct a wide range of activities, it can be difficult to compare them in any meaningful fashion. To guide the selection of a pool of comparable survey participants from these highly variable organizations, a working definition of a DHC and selection criteria were developed.

The working definition was developed after examining several dozen organizations that define themselves as DHCs (or have been defined by others as such) and identifying their missions and the range of activities that fall under their purview. In crafting this definition, the following assumptions were made:

- A "center" implies a central (physical or virtual, or both) area where a suite of activities is conducted by individuals dedicated to a common mission.
- "Digital humanities" implies humanities-based research, teaching, and intellectual engagement conducted with digital technologies and resources. The use of these technologies may be prosaic (e.g., using new media to conduct humanities research or enhance teaching) or transformative (e.g., developing wholly new products and processes that transform existing knowledge and create new scholarship).

Working from these assumptions, and from knowledge of the vast array of activities undertaken by DHCs, the following working definition was developed:

> A digital humanities center is an entity where new media and technologies are used for humanities-based research, teaching, and intellectual engagement and experimentation. The goals of the center are to further humanities scholarship, create new forms of knowledge, and explore technology's impact on humanities-based disciplines. To accomplish these goals, a digital humanities center undertakes some or all of the following activities:
>
> - builds digital collections as scholarly or teaching resources;
> - creates tools for
>   - authoring (i.e., creating multimedia products and applications with minimal technical knowledge or training)
>   - building digital collections
>   - analyzing humanities collections, data, or research processes
>   - managing the research process;
> - uses digital collections and analytical tools to generate new intellectual products;
> - offers digital humanities training (in the form of workshops, courses, academic degree programs, postgraduate and faculty training, fellowships, and internships);

- offers lectures, programs, conferences, or seminars on digital humanities topics for general or academic audiences;
- has its own academic appointments and staffing (i.e., staff does not rely solely on faculty located in another academic department);
- provides collegial support for, and collaboration with, members of other academic departments within the DHC's home institution (e.g., offers free or fee-based consultation services; enters into collaborative projects with other campus departments);
- provides collegial support for, and collaboration with, members of other academic departments, organizations, or projects *outside* the DHC's home institution (e.g., offers free or fee-based consultation to outside groups; enters into collaborative projects with external groups);
- conducts research in humanities and humanities computing (digital scholarship);
- creates a zone of experimentation and innovation for humanists;
- serves as an information portal for a particular humanities discipline;
- serves as a repository for humanities-based digital collections (e.g., Web sites, electronic text projects, QuickTime movie clips);
- provides technology solutions to humanities departments (e.g., serves an information technology (IT) role for humanities departments).

2.2 Identifying and Selecting Survey Participants

Dozens of survey candidates were identified from a variety of sources (see Appendix A). Several criteria were used to cull a usable sample from these candidates. Only U.S.-based DHCs were considered because of time and logistical constraints. In addition, the following groups were excluded from consideration:

- Digital projects. While DHCs often develop and support digital projects, projects developed and supported by entrepreneurial individuals independent of the auspices of a center were excluded from consideration.
- Libraries, academic departments, or other institutions that function solely as repositories for digital humanities collections.
- Academic departments that offer a degree-granting program in digital humanities or related areas (such as digital media design or humanities informatics) but do not conduct any other activities (listed above) common to DHCs.
- Digital libraries (collections of digital resources) or digital library research centers (organizations that develop methods for scanning, ingesting, or otherwise moving print materials to digital form).

Although all these organizations, departments, and projects may be critical components of a humanities center, their singular focus excludes them from being considered a DHC under the working definition developed above.

The remaining candidates were assessed using the working definition as a guideline. Organizations whose missions and goals were consistent with this definition and whose activities included four or more of the most frequent activities conducted by DHCs were selected as survey candidates. These organizations were contacted and asked to participate in the survey. Thirty-two organizations agreed to take part (see Appendix B).

3. Survey Methodology

3.1 Methodology

The survey methodology was influenced by the project timeframe, logistics, and the nature of information that was sought. The project team had only nine months to contact and survey 32 geographically dispersed organizations, analyze the responses, and summarize the results. Because of the number of organizations, site visits were not possible within this limited period of time. At the same time, the number of participating organizations was too small to make a traditional U.S. mail, e-mail, or online survey format practicable. In addition, many of the lines of inquiry proposed could not be pursued in the succinct manner characteristic of the questionnaire format used in traditional mail or e-mail surveys. Questions about business models or collaborations, for example, require a level of discussion and follow-up that are not possible in self-administered survey instruments.

Given the factors cited above, it was decided that the most expedient method for conducting the survey would be a two-pronged approach that involved (1) gathering relevant information from DHC Web sites and publications, and (2) conducting phone interviews with center directors (or their high-level designates). This combined "review/interview" strategy made the best use of the project timeframe and of the directors' and interviewer's time. The interviewer obtained much of the needed background and operational information about DHCs from their Web sites and from articles, press releases, and other online resources. The phone interviews themselves could therefore be devoted to focused and nuanced discussions of issues such as DHC business models or decision-making processes, which are typically not covered in print or online resources.

3.2 Survey Areas

Several factors influenced the survey topics and questions. Key considerations were the project's goals and the types of information that might be useful for the participants of SCI 6. The selection of topics was further influenced by discussions about critical information areas that warranted exploration that took place with various individuals during Phase I, and by a review of print and Web resources that explored issues in digital humanities computing and DHCs. In the end, the survey focused on six topics:

1. general background information
2. governance
3. administration
4. operations
5. sustainability
6. partnerships and collaborations

In each of these areas, a specific set of information was identified as critical to the understanding of issues or providing context. Questions were developed to derive this information, and a template was created to guide the research process and phone interviews (see Appendix C).

3.3 A Note about Confidentiality

Individuals who took part in the phone interviews on behalf of the centers were guaranteed confidentiality to encourage candid discussion. As a result, all findings are reported here anonymously or in aggregated fashion, unless the information was available in a publication or on the center's Web site.

Sometimes findings are reported in a generalized fashion (e.g., "many" or "most"), but in other instances more detail (e.g., number or percentage of centers) is given. The decision to report one way or another depended on the following factors:

Confidentiality: When specificity might inadvertently reveal the identity of a center (for example, when percentages were so skewed that the identify of a minority center might be obvious to readers), the results were reported in a generalized fashion to preserve the anonymity of the center.

Complexity of answers: When questions that had been presumed to yield "yes/no" answers proved to be more complex than anticipated ("Yes, but ..."), results were reported in a generalized manner. Descriptions and examples are presented to illustrate the nature of issues that yielded such responses.

4. Survey Findings

4.1 General Background

4.1.1 Physical and Virtual Locations

All the DHCs in the survey have physical and virtual locations, but some centers are more rooted to the "brick and mortar" than others because of the nature of their activities, operations, and governance. Consortia and membership-based centers (such as the Multimedia

Education Resource for Learning and Online Teaching [MERLOT] or the Humanities, Arts, Science, and Technology Advanced Collaboratory [HASTAC]), by contrast, operate largely through virtual space because their members are geographically dispersed and can gain access to primary resources only in this manner. These centers' facilities are used largely by the administrative and technical staff who manage the centers rather than by the members or partners.

University-based centers do not have the issue of dispersed memberships who need access to common resources because the centers' primary partners (researchers, staff, and students) are located within physical proximity of each other. While activities take place in both the physical and virtual locations, the physical site is more than an administrative office or server location: it is the hub of the center's activities.

4.1.2 Research Domains

Some DHCs address the full range of humanities disciplines, while others focus on one or more humanities discipline(s) that form the core of their scholarly or pedagogical pursuits (e.g., design and culture in Islamic societies). The research domains of the surveyed centers can be categorized as follows:

The humanities (and beyond): Centers whose research domains encompass all of the humanities (and frequently the interstitial areas between the humanities), the social and natural sciences, the arts, and technology. Many are interested in crossing the boundaries between these areas to address what one center characterized as "the big human questions."

Discipline-specific: Centers that focus on particular disciplines within the humanities or social sciences, or both, such as history, English, literature, art history, or architecture.

Humanities pedagogy: Centers concerned with teaching and instructional methods for learning in the humanities. These centers may have a specific disciplinary focus (e.g., teaching languages or history) or may explore aspects of pedagogy in digital environments (e.g., writing and literacy in new media environments).

Experimentation: Centers that explore new methods of creativity or that challenge existing notions about cultural products in a digital arena. These centers develop and nurture experimental or experiential activities in such areas as digital art and performance, the changing nature of literacy in a networked culture, or re-envisioning the book in a digital environment.

Although DHCs may emphasize one domain, it is the nature of the humanities enterprise that nearly all venture into other areas at some point. A center with a discipline-specific domain, for example, may incorporate pedagogical components into its projects (e.g., using technology to teach history). Conversely, a center whose focus is multimedia literacy may explore this area within the context of an undergraduate course in classics.

4.1.3 Founding Dates

The oldest center in the survey was founded in 1978, the newest in 2005. The mean year of founding for the sample is 1992; the median and mode are 1999. However, founding dates are misleading because they are based on different definitions of what activity marks a center's inception. Some DHCs mark their founding date as the year they received research center status at their university (i.e., the equivalent of their "incorporation"). Others use the date of the first digital humanities project that set them on the trajectory toward becoming a full-fledged center. The date for the oldest center in the survey reflects its founding as a traditional humanities center that has now undertaken digital humanities initiatives.

4.1.4 Founding History

Digital humanities centers arise from a variety of circumstances. Frequently, a single event launches a larger process that results in the formation of a center. One such event has been characterized as the "key discussion." Whether in the guise of a formal meeting or a casual conversation, many centers were formed because a faculty member discussed the idea with a receptive dean, a provost, or an outside funder who offered startup monies.

Grants have also been an impetus for the creation of centers, albeit indirectly. Many digital projects initially funded by grants developed beyond their original intent, generating other projects and activities. Eventually, a decision was made to organize all these activities under one formal structure (a "center") for greater strategic management.

Some centers emerged from a campus-wide humanities or pedagogy initiative. These initiatives came from the highest administrative levels of the university (often the office of the president), and included a DHC as one component of a broader strategy to promote the humanities on campus.

Still other DHCs had their origins in computing service units within a university. Over time, campus IT centers or humanities computing facilities may have found themselves moving from a role as purveyors of technology services to incubators and managers of digital humanities projects. In time, their original purpose is subsumed by these other activities, and a restructuring occurs that acknowledges and sanctions their new role as a DHC.

The academic entrepreneur also plays a role in the startup of centers. HASTAC emerged in this way, as did the Perseus Digital Library. Equally important are the efforts of the prolific digital humanities scholar who initially organizes a center to meet his or her immediate needs but that, given the collaborative nature of digital humanities, organically grows to encompass the digital scholarship and research of others.

However, the reality behind the founding of DHCs is more complex than these circumstances imply. A grant, a strategic discussion, or an entrepreneurial individual may be a stimulus, but the process from idea to implementation is protracted and often occurs in an unstructured way rather than through any long-range planning. It is fueled and sustained through continual fund-raising, wider efforts to solicit buy-in around campus, and greater reaches that move the idea in a stepwise progression from project (singular activity) to program (long-term activity) to center (multiple activities).

4.1.5 Mission Statements

Convention dictates that mission statements should be short, jargon-free, and understandable by a lay reader. They also should address three questions:

1. What is the organization's purpose?
2. How does it achieve this purpose?
3. What principles or values guide its work?

DHC mission statements do not always adhere to these guidelines; instead, they represent an eclectic mix of content, form, and varying levels of clarity. They all address the purpose of their organization (Question 1), and most include descriptions of how they accomplish their work (Question 2). The principles or beliefs that guide DHCs (Question 3) are less frequently and less clearly expressed.

When one examines the mission statements in detail, a wide range of purposes (Question 1) is evident. DHCs want to do the following:

- create global communities of scholars, students, professionals, and the public engaged in humanities questions;
- share experience, resources, and dialogue;
- challenge or rethink traditional assumptions about learning, literacy, or print media;
- promote and advance disciplines, civic engagement, interdisciplinary research, creative uses of technology, and public understanding of humanities issues;
- explore the way digital technologies are changing scholarship, particularly in work processes and products;
- harness digital technologies for scholarship, teaching, and public service;
- provide funding, infrastructure, and technical assistance needed for digital humanities to thrive;
- become environments for experimentation (e.g., incubators or think tanks) that develop scholarly or pedagogical work and foster emerging fields;
- gain efficiencies by leveraging infrastructure and expertise;
- create tools, digital content, standards, research approaches and methodologies, learning and development environments, projects, and globally networked resources;
- bridge gaps between humanities, art, and scientific disciplines; pedagogy and technology; and technical innovation and humanities concerns;
- democratize and revitalize disciplines for diverse audiences; and
- collaborate across disciplinary "divides" (e.g., humanists, artists, and social scientists with computer scientists and engineers).

The centers achieve these goals (Question 2) through the following activities:

- providing resources (funding, staffing, tools, space, access to experts, publishing outlets) and support services (technical, grant-writing, administrative);
- offering opportunities for dialog (forums, lectures, presentations, events, conferences) and learning (courses, workshops, online training);
- developing and managing projects and research agendas;
- offering collaborative, partnership, and community-building opportunities;
- creating services, applications, networks, digital collections, and primary source materials;
- assessing technologies;
- conducting outreach to faculty, researchers, students, teachers, and the general public;
- consulting for the academy, industry, business and educational communities;
- serving as an intermediary for dispersed humanities activities; and
- preserving digital materials.

The principles and values that guide the centers' efforts (Question 3) were identified as follows:

The enduring value of the humanities, particularly faith in humanistic traditions and in the importance of the liberal arts; belief that the humanities have a vital contribution to make in the contemporary world; and honoring the rich legacy of culture.

Collaboration and cross-disciplinarity, particularly the importance of transcending divisions between the arts, sciences, and humanities; between the academy, industry, and culture; between practitioners and theorists; and the value of interdisciplinary research.

Openness, in the form of the free flow of ideas; transparency in work and practice; a progressive intellectual property system; and greater access to source material for the study of the humanities.

Civic and social responsibility, particularly, developing a citizenry of critical thinkers; presenting a democratic understanding of the past; emphasizing the importance of historical, visual, and multimedia literacy; reaching out to the general public; working with poorly resourced partners (e.g., organizations in developing nations); and understanding the social and political consequences of digital technology.

Questioning sacred cows by rethinking traditions and challenging assumptions, and according equal value to both theory and practice in digital humanities.

4.1.6 Constituencies

DHCs serve six major categories of constituents:
1. members of the university community, such as faculty, students (undergraduate and graduate), postdoctoral and faculty fellows, and administrators;

2. the broader research and scholarly community outside of the DHC's university or parent institution, such as visiting researchers or international scholars;

3. the education community, including K–12 teachers and students, as well as university instructors; this community often is divided further by discipline (history, science, and English teachers) or grade level (middle and high school teachers);

4. disciplines, professions, and professional interests, such as communities defined by discipline (classicists, linguists, historians), profession (artists, writers, or librarians), or mixed groups of professionals (e.g., architects, urban planners, designers and others interested in the built environment) brought together by a common interest;

5. corporate entities, such as cultural heritage institutions, research centers, international standards organizations, and business and industry; and

6. general public and community groups.

Some DHCs describe their respective constituencies broadly by their content focus (e.g., anyone who uses historical maps) or need (e.g., digital humanities practitioners who lack traditional support systems). Others (e.g., those interested in exploring the discourse in electronic literature) apply broader, more cerebral descriptions because they have found their constituency to be so diverse that it defies standard categorization.

4.2 Governance

Thirty of the DHCs surveyed are governed within a university infrastructure, and two are independent organizations. An important distinction exists between how a center is governed and how it operates. Two of the university-governed centers *operate* as membership DHCs, i.e., they run a large digital repository of content for a special community of members who have a common interest in the resources of the repository. The members help in the operation of the center (e.g., by contributing content, serving on committees and editorial boards that vet resources, or managing projects). However, these centers are largely *governed* by universities, not by the membership. Other centers are under the leadership of their founders; they operate in a university environment and receive in-kind support in the form of infrastructure, but are overseen by their founders with little apparent governance by university administration. With the exception of one independently governed DHC, all the centers surveyed are not-for-profit entities, or are housed within a larger nonprofit organization (e.g., a university).

4.2.1 Reporting Structure/Place on Organizational Chart

The directors of DHCs under university governance most often report to an academic or administrative dean of a school, college, or division at the university. The next most frequent "direct report" is to a university vice president or provost, followed by the chair or faculty of the department in which a center is physically located. One center is unusual in that its director has no formal reporting line but instead several staff report informally to various deans, a primary funder, and the university president. Another reports to the university's chief information officer. Of the two DHCs that are independent organizations, one director reports to a board of trustees, and the other to the center's funders.

In reality, most DHCs often have primary, secondary, and unofficial reporting lines. They may, for example, officially report to their department chair and indirectly report to the dean of their college. Those who report to a dean may also have a special reporting arrangement with the provost. Some centers split reporting between academic and administrative deans because the work of the center has financial or programmatic ties to both groups. A surprising number of centers have, in addition to their formal reporting requirements, loose or nominal arrangements of courtesy reporting to campus administrators and departments.

For centers operating in a university environment, the location of the center on the university's organizational chart is often determined by the circumstances of its origin. If a center was created within an academic department, it is usually located with that department on an organizational chart. If its genesis was among partnering faculty located in different departments, the center may be placed at a higher level, within a college or school or division. Multicampus units may fall under the chancellor's office of the university system or the office of the president on the campus where the DHC physically resides.

Seven centers have been relocated on their university's organizational chart at some point in their history. Sometimes the change was brought about by the center's own growth: as the center grew, it began encroaching too heavily upon the resources of its original home unit (an academic department, for example), and thus was moved under the administration of another, larger-resourced area of the university. In a few cases, centers were moved as part of university-wide restructuring.

Centers located in universities are referred to under many different administrative categories by their parent organization. They may be labeled a "program," an "independent unit," or a "unit" within a particular department; a "research program," an "independent research center," or an "organized research unit" within a particular school; a "research center/program/lab" or "center" at the university; or a "multicampus unit" in a state university system. Interestingly, some DHCs can be located neither from a search of their university's Web home page nor on the pages of the site that list university departments, units, and programs. Digital humanities centers that do appear on such lists usually are labeled as "research centers" or "research programs."

4.2.2 Ancillary Groups Involved in Governance

In addition to being subject to governance of individuals, departments, or schools, DHCs are often subject to oversight by ancillary groups. These groups provide assistance in the form of advice or review, oversight of budgets and programs, or disciplinary expertise.

Ancillary governing groups go by many names (e.g., advisory councils, steering committees, administrative boards) but perform duties in the following areas:

- providing advice on planning, policy decisions, and ad hoc issues;
- serving on grant-selection and review committees;
- fund-raising;
- representing DHC programs around campus;
- reviewing programs, budgets, and progress on projects;
- providing feedback from faculty;
- clarifying the DHC's mission and activities; and.
- brainstorming ideas, projects, and research areas.

The groups may be convened on an ad hoc basis (the norm) or at regular intervals. Members may be formally appointed to serve by a dean or provost or informally selected by the DHC director and staff. For official appointments, a DHC director may make recommendations to the senior official who is responsible for the appointments.

Individuals who serve on these groups are often selected on the basis of their involvement in the center (e.g., past partners, members, current staff). However, it is equally common to find members with no prior center affiliation. Such individuals are selected because they have the disciplinary expertise, financial acumen, or administrative experience that the center lacks.

Terms of service for members of these groups tend to be open ended. Only seven DHCs have term limits—ranging from one to five years—for their committees. Members generally serve until they choose to resign.

4.3 Administration

Unlike governance, administration focuses on the day-to-day operations of an organization. These operations are conducted by a center director and staff rather than overseeing groups. In the case of consortia or membership-based DHCs, members also may assist in these administrative duties.

4.3.1 Staffing

Determining DHC staffing levels is an inexact undertaking. While the number of staff at a center may range from 2 to 51 individuals, DHCs count their staff in different ways. Some include undergraduate and graduate students, especially when these individuals are responsible for large portions of a center's work. Others include only full-time staff, and still others count faculty who are only loosely affiliated with the center. The numbers also fluctuate greatly from year to year because many positions are funded by soft money.

Staff positions are found in the following areas:

Business and Administration
—Office managers, administrative assistants
—Business managers, accountants, chief financial officers
—Development officer and grant administrators
—Communications and publicity staff

Center Management
—Directors, codirectors, and associate, assistant and executive directors
—Project managers and coordinators

Content Production
—Producers, production assistants
—Content developers, writers
—Creative directors, content directors
—Film, video, and audio managers

Education and Outreach
—Coordinators of educational and professional development programs
—Directors of educational partnerships and planning
—Directors of assessment, outreach, and marketing of educational programs and services
—Directors of academic programs
—Education technology coordinators (crossover with IT positions)
—Education consultants

Facilities Management
—Building and operations managers and staff

Information Technology
—Coordinators of academic technology, Internet development
—Chief technology officers, technology directors
—Systems programmers, software engineers, database administrators, information architects
—Web site developers, Webmasters, Web application developers
—Providers of instructional support or client services; managers of new media labs, technology "evangelists"

Library, Archives, and Information Science
—Traditional and digital librarians
—Metadata specialists and catalogers
—Audio and digital archivists
—Digital media producers

Research and Scholarship
—Scholars, curators, visiting researchers and professors, research associates
—Directors or coordinators of research projects or fellowships programs

Publishing
—Editors, managing editors, Web editors, copyeditors, review editors

Miscellaneous
—Student assistants assigned to various roles as needed

Staff positions are funded in a variety of ways. Graduate student labor may be supported by an assistantship from the student's academic department, or may be a "joint share" between the center and the department. At state universities, staff members often are state employees and are paid through state budget lines. Some center staff members are funded entirely by other departments, projects, grants, or special discretionary funds provided by university administration. For centers located within an academic department, staff members may be shared by agreement between the department chair and the center director.

A small number of center staff work from remote locations. One DHC's entire programming team is distributed around the United States and Eastern Europe. Another center has staff members located in countries where it has its international programs.

4.3.2 Reporting Structures

DHCs reporting structures are determined largely by the number of staff and the range of programming. Such structures are of two major types. Centers with relatively small staffs and a more singular program focus have a less formal structure, with staff reporting directly to the center director or assistant director.

Centers with midsize to large staffs and diverse programming have a hierarchical reporting structure in which lower-level staff report to middle- or upper-level staff who, in turn, report to the director. Staff in the middle reporting layer may be divided by service area (e.g., network services report to a chief technology officer), by function (e.g., programmers report to a head programmer), by project area (e.g., project staff report to a project manager), or by an incremental series of reporting levels (e.g., teams report to team leaders, team leaders report to an assistant director, and the assistant director reports to a director). Some centers have codirectors who share management duties and provide coverage for one another during travel periods or sabbaticals. A significant amount of "dotted-line" reporting also takes place between directors and the chair or faculty of academic departments participating in DHC projects.

However, even the most rigid reporting structures have some measure of fluidity. For example, staff may sidestep their direct-report levels if they have an administrative issue, or they may have opportunities (such as staff meetings) where they report directly to upper management. One DHC characterized its reporting structure as a "soft hierarchy" because the official university reporting lines were not rigidly applied by the center.

4.3.3 Shared Appointments
Academic Faculty

Ninety-two percent of university-based centers have staff with faculty appointments in other academic departments. These appointments may be in traditional humanities departments, the social sciences, engineering departments, and the arts. (For a full list of departments affiliated with centers in this survey, see Appendix

D.) Most of these appointments include teaching, research, and administrative responsibilities within the faculty members' respective departments.

Of 47 joint positions identified, 88 percent are fully funded by the academic department (not the center). The academic department usually offers joint appointees some form of compensation for the extra duties they assume on behalf of the centers. The most frequent form of compensation is release time from teaching. Release time may be apportioned by percentage (i.e., 50 percent teaching, 50 percent center work) or by courseload reductions that vary from one course every second year to one course every semester. Other forms of compensation include summer compensation, overload compensation, and stipends. Compensation arrangements are negotiated individually and can vary within departments. Center directors, for example, may receive more release time than other joint appointees at a center.

Presumably, those departments that offer some form of compensation to joint appointees do so because they value the appointees' work at the center. However, not all departments are so generous: a few allow teaching-release time only if the joint appointee can compensate the department for his or her unavailability (which can sometimes be done using center or grant funds). One center turns the tables even further, by requiring its staff (who are center funded) to give their teaching monies to the center to offset the loss of their time on center activities.

A small number of joint appointees receive no allowances whatsoever for their dual department/center duties. These individuals agree to the extra workloads because they believe their scholarly interests and the interests of the center are best served by their involvement. Compensation comes in the form of the intangible rewards they receive for teaching, research, and scholarship.

Joint center/academic department appointments are often specified in contracts that may be reconsidered at various intervals. Tenure-track faculty, for example, may request that their contracts reflect more teaching and less center work as they approach their tenure-decision year. Similarly, a center and academic departments may alter their entire compensation formula for faculty as the center's offerings gain traction and additional faculty time is required by the center.

Administrative Faculty

Although rarer than academic faculty appointments, shared appointments also occur between the centers and various administrative departments and research centers. Administrative faculty, such as deans or library directors, may have full or provisional affiliations with centers. Senior scholars and research scientists (the latter often from campus computing centers) may also have joint arrangements. Because these individuals usually do not have teaching responsibilities, course-release time does not figure into the equation. Instead, these positions are supported by the administrative department or research center, or by a cost share between the center and the depart-ment/research center.

4.4 Operations

A center's operations include the activities it undertakes, the deci-sion-making processes it undergoes, and the measures it uses to as-sess its work. An understanding of center operations clarifies how the center is run and managed, and the issues it encounters as it strives to implement its agenda.

4.4.1 Activities

Digital humanities centers undertake the following range of activities.

Events

Centers develop and host events such as lectures, conferences, semi-nars, or performances for the purposes of fostering collegial relation-ships and promoting discourse. Events may address humanities themes or technological developments. Although some events (such as conferences) are intended for a specific professional community, many are open to entire university communities and often the gen-eral public as well.

Product Development

The products developed by DHCs range from traditional materials, such as print publications, to less-tangible items, such as virtual en-vironments. To gain insight into the wide range of products DHCs offer, it is useful to organize them by function:

- *Teaching materials and resources*, such as online repositories of learn-ing materials, teacher "toolboxes," and online tutorials on various technology topics;
- *Digital workspaces*, such as wikis, blogs, and virtual environments used for teaching, creating art, or exploring virtual worlds. These workspaces use Web 2.0 tools that are developed by others but are offered by the centers to users for their project needs;
- *Publications*, such as online newsletters and e-journals, white papers and articles, textbooks, and guides on topics such as scan-ning, text encoding, and best practices for digital projects;
- *Tools*, such as plug-ins, conversion tools, authoring and organiza-tions tools, media annotation tools, and desktop versions of digital libraries; and
- *Miscellaneous products*, such as exhibits (physical and virtual), documentary videos, podcasts, and Webcasts.

Programs

Programs are long-term efforts that incorporate many singular ac-tivities for the purposes of a larger objective, such as the creation of a digital library, a collaboration, or a professional development cur-riculum. DHCs programs include:

- *Development and incentive programs*, such as workshops and seminars for teachers on how to bring scholarship, technology, and learning methods into the classroom; rewards programs that acknowledge individuals and groups whose contributions have furthered a disciplinary area or enhanced the work of a center; and seed grants to assist in the startup of digital humanities projects;
- *Digital humanities research projects*—projects that use innovative technologies and approaches in humanities research, such as 3-D modeling projects like the Digital Roman Forum;
- *Compilations for research and teaching,* such as the Willa Cather Archive and the Walt Whitman Archive;
- *Projects that explore technology for humanities teaching and learning,* such as the Visual Knowledge Project and the Learning Design Studio; and
- *Academic programs* that offer degrees, honors programs, research fellowships, and residency programs (See Section 4.4.2).

Services

Although DHCs do not define themselves as service organizations, a review of their offerings suggests that service plays a large role in their operations. These services include:

- *Consultation* to the academic, cultural, nonprofit, government, and corporate communities on issues as diverse as digitization, project management, and learning initiatives;
- *Facilities management* for new media and language learning laboratories, classrooms, and help desks;
- *Technical infrastructure support* for digitization in the field, building and maintaining hardware and software infrastructure for online communities, and designing and implementing digital laboratory environments;
- *Web and Internet support* such as hosting, storage space, site mirroring, and Web site development;
- *Preservation assistance,* such as archiving inactive projects, workspaces, or images; and developing migration plans,
- *Management and administration services,* such as project planning, brokering services, administrative support (office assistance and grant administration), and providing administrative "homes" to related groups;
- *Educational and pedagogical services,* such as assessments of curricula, teaching, and educational programming; staff development in humanities instructional methods; and course and curriculum design;
- *Technical assistance,* such as metadata encoding, digital resource design, statistical analysis, hardware/software support, media digitization, and prototyping new technologies;
- *Training* on the use of various multimedia, center-developed resources and materials and instructional technologies; and
- *Digital humanities expertise and advice* on national trends, best practices, and academic and peer review for digital humanities projects.

4.4.2 Teaching and Other Pedagogical Activities

Digital humanities centers strongly believe they have an obligation to nurture and train the next generation of digital humanities researchers, scholars, and professionals. Since the primary route for such training occurs in colleges and universities, pedagogical activities at this level are critical. Courses, degree programs, internships, graduate assistantships, and fellowships constitute the building blocks of a larger effort to train individuals in digital humanities scholarship.

Academic Programs

Four of the DHCs surveyed offer degrees in some aspect of digital humanities, but only one is a full degree-granting program (awarding B.F.A. and Ph.D. degrees in digital arts and experimental media). Two other centers offer certificate or equivalent programs (in humanities computing) that must be taken in conjunction with a regular graduate program, and one center offers an undergraduate cross-campus honors program (in multimedia scholarship), taken in conjunction with a regular undergraduate disciplinary major.

The apparent paucity of degree-granting programs among DHCs is largely a function of sampling bias: degree-granting programs that did not conduct any of the other activities outlined in this study's definition of a digital humanities center (see Section 2.1) were excluded from the survey. In addition, universities traditionally allow academic departments (not research centers) to grant degrees. A few centers are working around this limitation by assisting academic departments with interdepartmental degree programs or by developing a certificate program in conjunction with an academic department.

Courses

Center faculty and staff develop and teach a prodigious number of courses in digital humanities topics. Some staff members are involved in developing courses for their university's new digital humanities degree programs, since they cannot offer such programs themselves. Others develop and teach courses on humanities computing in a specific discipline, such as multimedia writing in an English department, or archaeological geometrics in a classics department. Still others are working to incorporate informatics training into the general undergraduate curriculum by integrating multimedia authoring skills into required undergraduate courses.

Academic departments increasingly recognize the importance of digital humanities to the skill set of their graduate students and are now including one or more courses on humanities computing in their graduate degree requirements. Courses on digital history theory and practice, digital scholarship, and digital technology for humanities research were among those cited as required for graduate student training in humanities disciplines ranging from history to American studies to archaeology to architecture.

Centers are also developing faculty training programs on integrating digital resources and technology into teaching and learning. These programs tend to be informal workshops or one-on-one training.

Internships
Forty-one percent of DHCs offer internships to undergraduate or graduate students, or both. Most are formal opportunities that include academic credit and/or pay, require a certain number of work hours, and assign the intern to a particular project or researcher (the latter in a mentor relationship). Informal internships are those in which the DHC hires a student in a role that they define as "intern-like" (i.e., the student learns about digital humanities on the job) but that has no formal program guidelines or selection processes.

Graduate Assistantships
Although fewer DHCs (19 percent) offer graduate assistantships than internships, this probably reflects the tradition of assistantships being awarded through academic departments and not research centers. (The centers that do offer assistantships usually base them in academic departments.) However, even when a center does not offer its own graduate assistantships, it often is populated with graduate students who are supported by assistantships from other academic departments. These departments agree to such an arrangement because it gives their students an opportunity to receive digital humanities training that the department cannot provide.

Fellowships
Fifty-six percent of DHCs offer fellowship opportunities to individuals at the graduate, postdoctoral, or mid- to senior-faculty level, or to those in other professions conducting work in the digital humanities. Fellowship periods may range from a few days to three years. The fellowships may be used to support dissertation research, project development, teaching, and participation in collaborative projects. Compensation varies widely, and may include monetary support, access to technology and technical support, travel monies, teaching-release time, research assistants, housing offsets, and administrative and grant writing support. While most fellowships are restricted to graduate students, postdocs, or other academics, a small but growing number are being made available to nonacademic professionals, such as librarians or artists who collaborate with digital humanities scholars.

Some DHCs do not offer fellowships but instead host "fellows" funded by other departments or institutions. These individuals choose to use their fellowship monies at the center because it offers them resources relevant to their particular fellowship projects.

Other Learning/Training Opportunities
Centers also offer learning opportunities distinct from the traditional offerings of internships, assistantships, and fellowships. Most of these opportunities are in the form of workshops and training pro-

grams held within a university community or taken on the road for K–12 educational communities. One nationwide competitive workshop offers early career (pretenure) scholars an opportunity to present their work for critical evaluation by senior scholars in the digital humanities.

Other opportunities include independent study courses for graduate and undergraduate students, residencies for artists and writers, and one-on-one tutoring and consultation with faculty and researchers. Some DHCs are creating learning opportunities outside of academia that may be nurturing the next generation of digital humanities scholars much earlier than ever before: in one instance, by offering internships to students at a local science-and-technology high school; in another, by bringing inner-city students to the center to learn about innovative uses of technology.

4.4.3 Decision Making

Deciding what projects and programs to develop is a key function of DHC management. Some centers make these decisions through a formal process that has a competitive selection-and-evaluation component. However, most decision making is informal, based on perceived needs, qualitative criteria, and local circumstances.

Informal Decision Making

Project and program ideas come to the attention of centers in ways that reflect a mix of opportunism, interest, and serendipity. A center may be approached by a faculty member or researcher, or a project may arise from within the center as a natural outgrowth of an existing project or a staff member's interests. Centers also actively solicit projects that come to their attention, or make strategic solicitations in which they identify grant opportunities, faculty who could benefit from their services, or courses that are ripe for a center's offerings. Politics may also enter the picture when a center is urged to consider a project by its university administration or a foundation.

The review process for informally assessed projects includes considerations of mission, staffing, budget, and potential. The following are some of the specific criteria cited by survey respondents:

- *Project "fit"*: Does the project mesh with the center's mission? Does it further the center's research agenda? Does it offer synergies with other center projects? Do the project's needs (e.g., technology, expertise) meet the center's offerings?
- *Center resources*: Does the center have the necessary resources, such as funding, space, and technologies, to undertake the project?
- *Project potential*: Does the project enable digital scholarship? How does it do so (e.g., through the creation of a tool or an archive)? Does it have the potential to build connections to other projects and researchers?
- *Bona fides of the principal investigator (PI)*: Does the PI bring the necessary knowledge and skills to the table? Does he or she have a record of success and a good reputation?
- *Funding potential*: Does the project have funding or funding potential?

Digital humanities centers get answers to these and other questions through extensive discussions with the project's PI. Final decisions are usually made by the DHC director or by consensus of core center staff. When a decision is made to proceed and funding is not available, initial efforts are spent procuring funding from diverse sources, including private donors, university discretionary funds, center funds, grants, and foundations. Most centers offer grant-writing support, and some even create prototypes to demonstrate the project's potential to funders. While centers rarely provide full funding from their own coffers, one DHC undertakes what it termed "speculative investing," agreeing to spend money up-front to develop a pilot project with the assumption that doing so will help deliver larger sums of money to sustain the project further.

Like funding, staffing for new projects comes from mixed sources. A center may assign its own staff to the project, or use its connections to pool the services of others, such as students, faculty, or computing center staff. Projects may also come with existing staff. In the end, staffing levels depend on resources at hand—both human and financial.

Formal Decision Making

Formal decision making is conducted on two types of programs: grants and fellowships. DHC grant programs are funded by a center's parent university or by foundations that give the center funds to offer "regrants" for special projects (such as seed grants to help projects get started or grants to develop conferences or seminars). Fellowships are usually foundation funded, although some centers report funding contributions from alumni or endowment funds.

Applying for either program is a competitive process, with centers issuing official announcements calling for applications. Selection committees then review the applications, applying certain criteria to their selection process. For grants and digital humanities fellowships, these criteria include assessments of the following:
- quality of proposal (in definition, organization, clarity, scope); and
- quality of candidate
  - likelihood of success
  - technology needs
  - research merit
  - innovativeness.

Less official, but no less important, considerations are:
- Does the applicant have agency in the project? Will he or she be an active participant and not expect the center to do the work?
- Why does the project need the center?
- Does the project fill a gap in the center's own research agenda?

4.4.4 Measuring Success

DHCs use qualitative and quantitative criteria to measure the success of their programs. The information they compile is used to gauge how well the center is addressing its mission and mandate, to produce evidence of a successful track record for grant agencies and fund-raising, to justify student technology fees, and to raise their social capital within its parent institution.

Success is measured both for projects and for the overall offerings of the center. Grant-funded projects receive more stringent assessments because funding agencies require evaluations at various points in a project's life cycle. Projects that are not funded by grants are generally assessed less frequently and less formally.

Criteria Used to Assess Individual Projects

Qualitative Criteria

- Did the project achieve its goals as specified in proposals and work plans? Is it on time, within budget, and doing what it set out to do?
- Was the project able to get external funding after the initial development period?
- Is the project being cited? Do others perceive it in a positive light?
- Is education being enhanced? Are the outputs being used to teach others?
- Is the project moving the broader digital humanities agenda forward? Is the project becoming a model for future work?
- Are partners pleased with the outcome?
- Can the project be leveraged into another project?
- Is the project or its resources being used in institutional initiatives?
- What are the project's spin-offs (e.g., tools, collaborations, contracts)?

Quantitative Criteria

- Results of surveys, user feedback, focus groups (especially for K–12 projects or products), entry/exit interviews
- Event attendance figures
- Number of applications or proposals received
- Number of publications arising from a project
- Amount of data captured or markup undertaken
- Number of program participants
- For online projects:
    - Number of site visits and unique visits
    - Geographic distribution of users
    - Number and length of page views
    - Number of downloads (for tools, products, etc.)
    - Number of daily users

Criteria Used to Assess the Overall Success of the Center

Qualitative Criteria

- The caliber of students, researchers, and faculty applying to the center
- The success of students who work at the center (e.g., their job offers, achievement of tenure)

- Are people actively seeking out the center for its offerings?

Quantitative Criteria
- Number of rewards received by center faculty, researchers, staff, and students
- Time to degree (for centers that offer academic programs)
- Course enrollment for center-developed classes
- Lab-usage statistics
- Member participation (for consortia)

Centers generally evaluate themselves, although a few are evaluated by independent review committees at their universities. Centers also conduct evaluations for grant-funded projects according to criteria required by each grant agency. Representatives of such centers feel these required evaluations are useful for measuring the success of individual programs; however, they cannot use these evaluations to measure success across all their programs because each funding agency has its own evaluation criteria.

4.4.5 How DHC Resources Are Used
Digital humanities centers often do not know the full extent of how their resources are used because they do not, or cannot, track this information in a consistent manner. Instead, they characterize use of their resources by communities. Scholars and researchers, for example, use the resources for research, publication, and scholarly engagement. Undergraduate and graduate students and postdoctoral fellows rely on them for research and training in areas not normally offered by their own academic programs. The university community takes advantage of DHC resources for courses, training, technology-enabled teaching facilities, and expertise in humanities computing, and often embeds DHC resources or services into broader university programs.

Teachers not only use the resources for developing K–12 curricula but also rely on them for professional development opportunities. College- and university-level instructors value DHC resources for teaching undergraduates about the use of technology in the humanities, and are using technology-based approaches to teach writing, fine arts, and history.

Members of the artistic community (particularly visual and performing artists and writers) incorporate DHC resources into their work, or use centers as places to develop and demonstrate their creative output. Professional communities of librarians, architects, urban planners, and software developers also participate in DHC programs for research. Cultural heritage organizations increasingly partner with centers on projects that require the use of their object collections.

While the groups cited above constitute the majority of DHC users, a significant number of centers consider the general public and local, regional, and statewide citizenry among their user base. As centers develop more community resources and actively engage interested members of the public in their research collection and community history projects, this user base continues to grow. But it is difficult to know how the general public is using Web-based projects.

4.4.6 Monitoring Usage

Usage is a key measure of success, but is extremely difficult to gauge for most DHC products and projects. Although some centers take care to collect usage information for each of their products and projects, such vigilance is not the norm. Centers often cite time or resource constraints as limiting their ability to monitor usage.

When usage is monitored, it is done most frequently on Web projects or events because usage statistics can be easily collected on these activities. Centers that develop community-based digital resources often monitor the amount of new material added to the resource by users, and then use this as a measure of growth and community engagement. Digital humanities centers that teach courses or monitor lab facilities may also monitor enrollment or facilities usage.

Usage figures made available during DHC interviews were impressive: for some Web resources, millions of visits per year; for registered resources, tens of thousands of registered users; and for courses and facilities usage, dozens of classes, with some centers reporting total yearly enrollment figures in the thousands. It is futile to compare usage statistics across centers because monitoring mechanisms are so variable. However, these numbers are useful for internal center assessments because they provide evidence of activity and help centers in their decision making.

4.4.7 Preservation Plans

As DHCs develop and accumulate digital content, preservation is receiving greater attention. While a few centers report that they have no preservation plan (or shift the responsibility for preservation to content owners or principal investigators), most do acknowledge their obligation to preserve the process and results of their digital scholarship, and they are addressing the issue in various ways. The centers most concerned about the issue are entering into agreements with preservation partners—institutions with expertise and experience in digital preservation. Libraries and statewide digital library initiatives (such as the California Digital Library) currently are the partners of choice. Some DHCs are investigating open-source repository solutions such as DSpace, while others are considering commercial vendors to outsource their hosting and archiving responsibilities. One DHC is working with several preservation partners, each of which was chosen for its interest in a particular digital resource of the center.

DHCs are also implementing a number of strategies to preserve their digital resources locally until they can identify a preservation partner or develop a more robust internal preservation plan. Some of these strategies include the following:

- educating partners, students, faculty, and researchers that preservation must be considered in project design and development;

- running "live" applications as long as possible;
- implementing a LOCKSS ("Lots of copies keep stuff safe") approach of distributing static copies of digital resources as widely as possible;
- establishing mirror sites;
- keeping archival versions on the center's intranet;
- making model outputs of the resource available in multiple, ubiquitous forms;
- migrating the resource to new hardware and software as older platforms become obsolete;
- offering licensed users a full copy of the resource in the event that the center becomes defunct or is unable to maintain the resource;
- separating production versions of resources from research versions, and placing production versions and services into a digital repository; and
- bundling past projects and data into current projects.

A few centers have incorporated digital preservation into their research agendas. Two centers that participated in this survey are working with partners to develop tools and technologies for archiving virtual worlds. One center is using its students' digital projects as a test bed in a collaborative project to develop archival methods for digital and experimental art. Still another is creating a digital repository for one of its oldest and most successful resources, and is hiring a digital archivist to extend this effort and make it scalable for the center's other resources.

4.4.8 Intellectual Property

Digital humanities centers are unanimous in their efforts to make their work transparent while respecting the intellectual property (IP) rights of others, a perspective borne out of their research and teaching mission. Most have some semblance of IP policy embedded within Web site usage statements or in their licenses or user agreements. A few are working to formalize these policies and to raise their profile among center staff and users.

Nearly all DHCs allow the researchers and scholars who contribute to the center's activities, or who develop digital products while working at the center, to retain the IP rights in their work. However, these individuals and center staff are responsible for procuring rights to content created by others (referred to as "third-party IP") that they use in their research. The centers require all those who create content under their auspices to grant them a royalty-free, nonexclusive, perpetual license to use the content for noncommercial purposes.

Beyond these efforts, the methods used to address IP scenarios range from none ("It has not been a problem") to a "case-by-case" handling of issues as they arise to a pre-emptive approach that uses legal instruments (e.g., release forms, partner agreements, and product licenses) to clarify IP issues in various contexts. One DHC with an active publication program has created a separate nonprofit arm to keep the ownership of copyrights clear and to maintain control over products (e.g., textbooks, documentaries, and Web resources) that generate sales and royalties. A few other DHCs are considering a similar model as rights issues become more difficult to handle internally.

As DHCs strive to make their work more accessible, they are incorporating open-source or partial rights schemes for their products (e.g., Creative Commons license). Some are moving away from, or avoiding, the commercial applications and partnerships they had pursued earlier because they found them to be too restrictive for research, teaching, and public use.

Paradoxically, DHCs are turning toward commercial applications to protect the IP rights of the third-party content used in so many of their programs and projects. Digital rights management (DRM) technologies such as watermarking, restrictions on full-text downloading of copyrighted works, and complex password-protection schemes are being used to safeguard against potential infringements. Digital humanities centers using DRM mechanisms feel they are important to their content-contributing partners, who can enter agreements with some level of assurance that the centers are behaving responsibly.

Digital humanities centers are also implementing IP-education programs for faculty, researchers, staff, and other users of their materials. One center outlines IP issues and policies in its fellowship guidelines; another is incorporating copyright law, fair use discussions, and academic standards policies in the courses it offers. A few university-based centers are working with their law schools to teach students about the IP issues they need to consider as they create and develop their work at the centers.

4.5 Sustainability

Discussions of sustainability were far-reaching, and included questions about planning strategies, current and past business models, funding sources, and challenges that threaten sustainability. The purpose of this line of inquiry is to identify resources available, efforts undertaken, and plans in place that allow DHCs to operate for the long term.

4.5.1 Planning Efforts

For centers that did not arise from an administrative mandate, the biggest hurdle in early formation was outlining a "proof of concept" about why they were needed. Written proposals, official meetings, and applications for in-house startup funds or challenge grants provided opportunities for explaining the rationales, but very few centers undertook needs assessments or feasibility studies, which are standard planning tools used by startup organizations. Rather, the centers demonstrated need by identifying a confluence of circumstances that argued for centralization of activities in a "center."

Planning efforts turned more formal once the centers were established. Twelve centers have a long-range planning document, such as a strategic plan or business plan, that they use for managing their growth and sustainability. Others hold yearly retreats, self-study assessments, or university-mandated assessments, and report that they use the information from these activities for long-term planning. The centers that reported no formal long-range planning documents or activities are acutely aware that they need to turn their attention to these activities, and cite time constraints as the primary reason why they have not yet done so.

4.5.2 Funding Sources

Centers receive funding and support from myriad sources: corporations; foundations; federal endowments; government and state agencies; universities; private donations and gifts; monies from consulting, licensing, sales, and royalties; and income from their own endowments.

Business and industry provide startup funds, hardware, and conference sponsorship, as well as in-kind assistance such as the use of broadband technology or nodes on corporate mainframes. Supporters in this category include well-known vendors from the software and hardware industry (e.g., Apple, SUN, IBM) and less obvious sponsors from the automobile, pharmaceutical, and publishing industries.

Foundation support usually takes the form of grants for specific center projects, although startup, maintenance, and bridging funds are not uncommon. Foundations also support fellowships, training programs, seminars, matching gifts, and publications. Foundation support comes from philanthropies with large endowments as well as from small, family-run trusts targeted to local community activities.

Challenge grants from U.S. federal endowments and funding agencies have helped many centers get their start. These agencies are also crucial supporters of meetings and conferences, residency programs, development of new media facilities, tool creation, and individual digital projects. At the time this survey was conducted, the National Endowment for the Humanities' Digital Humanities Initiative was getting under way, and many centers mentioned their intent to apply to this program for digital humanities startup funds, challenge grants, workshops, and collaboration grants.

Other federal and state agencies are also important funding sources for DHCs. Various programs in the U.S. Department of Education have supported centers with pedagogical interests, and other, less obvious federal agencies (e.g., the Air Force Office of Scientific Research, the U.S. Agency for International Development, the State Department, and the Small Business Administration) have funded various center projects. Among state agencies, the major funding sources are arts and humanities councils that fund center projects associated with state communities. There are also larger state programs, such as the California Lottery Fund, that contribute general funds for higher education that get funneled down to centers in state university systems.

Because the majority of DHCs are located within universities, it is not surprising that universities are a key source of funding. Support comes directly in the form of annual budget lines, or less directly in the form of funding provided by individual schools or departments working with the centers (e.g., the School of Engineering, the Department of English). In addition to baseline operating funds or startup funds, universities frequently subsidize staff salaries, student support, and infrastructure (such as office space or technology). They may also provide centers with funds generated from the university's student technology fees.

An assortment of special interest groups and other revenue sources also contribute to center funding. Specialty groups (e.g., the American Quilt Alliance), professional associations (e.g., the Modern Languages Association), private donations and gifts, conference and event fees, consulting income, and royalties from sales and subscriptions play a role in DHC budgets. Although these sources contribute relatively small percentages to a center's annual income, in lean years (between grants or during budget cuts), they are often critical in easing cash flow problems.

Centers could only guess as to what percentage of their funding was received from various sources. Because their responses were ballpark estimates and because the centers used different baseline parameters to develop them, the funding could not be compared in any meaningful fashion. It is, however, certain that universities, followed by grants and foundations, are the most frequently cited funding sources for centers.

4.5.3 Business Models

Business models were discussed in the very narrow sense of finances, resources, and programs used by a center to maintain its operations. The models for university-based DHCs are complex, revealing a mixed calculus of support involving university budget lines and/or in-kind services and infrastructure, combined with some or all of the following: grants, consulting or licensing income, royalties, endowment income, faculty support, corporate support, student labor, and donations. The few centers that depart from this model include a membership-based DHC that relies on academic partners' fees and huge investments of volunteer labor from partner-members in addition to its "home" university's staff and infrastructure support; a membership DHC funded entirely by a philanthropy; and an independent center funded by grants and foundation support, endowment income, capital campaigns, and a formal gift program.

These business models are not unusual for what are essentially nonprofit research organizations. Perhaps more interesting than the models themselves are the novel efforts under way by centers to secure resources and expand the models. Some centers, for example, are negotiating unique arrangements with their parent university that leverage the centers' contributions to university-wide teaching endeavors. One DHC was able to secure funds from student tuition fees based on its involvement in creating a cross-campus undergraduate program. Another center negotiated full-time faculty commitment to the center (from an original formula of 50:50 split time) by offering the faculty's academic departments a guaranteed number of seats for their students in the center's most popular courses.

Other novel efforts to expand existing business models include, for one center, the establishment of a European office to provide a base for expanding and diversifying the funding pool. Another center has embarked on a pilot project with its university's academic technology department to identify ways to coordinate staff, efforts, and resources more effectively.

Twenty-one centers (66 percent) report that their current business models differ from earlier versions. When examined more closely, however, many of these changes are in degree rather than kind (e.g., fewer grants than in the past, more student labor, or more university funding). A truly substantial change in the model often occurs when a center matures and moves off its startup funds, which are running out, to the more diversified models that now exist.

Some centers change their operational models because they are not satisfactorily moving the center toward its programmatic goals, and these changes subsequently alter the business model. In one instance, a center operating as a seed grant or an incubator program decided to develop, and raise funds for, its own programs after determining that incubated projects would lie fallow once they left the center. Another DHC changed its university status from that of a research center to a research laboratory, a distinction that results in a more precarious funding model (the center must now raise grants for all programming) but that fits better with the center's mission and intent as a place for collaboration and experimentation.

Other business models change with growth or with downsizing. One membership-based DHC expanded its offerings beyond its original university system to a wider array of academic partners, forcing a reconsideration of both funding and governance. Another center originally served the broad academic community under a cost-center (i.e., fee for service) model, but was scaled back by its parent university during a period of fiscal crisis, and now serves only the university and operates within its funding structure.

4.5.4 Sustainability Challenges

Unstable funding is the primary issue threatening the sustainability of centers. Survey respondents noted that the entire U.S. funding system is shortsighted, citing its emphasis on projects, its tendency to be influenced by trends and interests of the moment, and the drastic funding fluctuations that can occur from one year to the next in state, local, and federal budgets. A funding infrastructure that focuses on the short term makes long-term sustainability difficult to achieve.

Instability of infrastructure was another concern, especially in a university context. University-based centers want a sustained commitment from their parent institutions that does not waver in times of fiscal crises, during changes in campus administration, or with the retirement or resignation of a center founder. This support needs to include direct budget lines as well as in-kind assistance.

Many centers are considering endowments as a way to overcome unstable funding and infrastructure. (Currently, only 22 percent of the centers surveyed have endowments, and they are generally modest.) Endowment income could decrease reliance on grants, help bridge the periods between grants, and protect against the vicissitudes of state and federal funding. Unfortunately, endowments are difficult for centers to develop. Universities often block the effort during their capital campaigns. Challenge grants designed to jumpstart endowment fund-raising lose traction as the grant becomes one of many overseen by university development offices. And soliciting private endowment contributions requires concerted fund-raising efforts that most centers are unable to sustain.

Staffing presents another concern. Universities pay below-market salaries, making it difficult to recruit and retain technical staff (such as Web developers or programmers) and entry-level administrative staff. There is also a shortage of Ph.D.s with the necessary humanities computing backgrounds to fill senior staff positions. When a center is fortunate enough to find appropriately trained Ph.D.s to fill its positions, they are frequently lured away by better offers within a few years' time.

As centers grow and mature, the importance of smooth management transitions is becoming apparent. In the absence of a transition plan, the departure of a center's founder or senior staff (through retirement, illness, or job offers) can jeopardize a center's position. A few centers that have gone through such events recall them as periods of great stress and uncertainty, with threats of closure, changes in oversight, and a paralysis in activities. Other centers whose leaders are slated to retire in the next few years expressed great apprehension about their future because they lack a transition plan.

Sustainability issues also surface with daily operations. Overextended work agendas, the amount of storage needed to accommodate the growing number and size of digital projects, and concerns about the future of individual projects are among the specific issues cited.

4.6 Partnerships

To explore the extent of collaborations, DHCs were asked how their partnerships are structured, whom they choose to partner with (and why), failed partnership experiences, and their ideas about the elements of a successful partnership.

4.6.1 Types of Partners and Partnerships

Digital humanities centers partner with individuals and groups in just about every community imaginable. Examples include the following:

- higher education (university schools, centers, departments, and faculty and students)

- K–12 teachers and schools
- funding organizations
- industry
- cultural heritage organizations
- community groups
- federal, state, and local municipalities
- professional associations
- nonacademic professionals (e.g., multimedia producers, artists, writers)
- nongovernmental organizations
- broadcast and print media (television, radio, newspaper)
- publishers
- general public

Sixty-three percent of the DHCs have international partnerships, and another 16 percent report having such partnerships "peripherally" through a faculty member or researcher's project. Eighty-one percent of centers both actively *seek out* partners and are approached by others who wish to partner with them. Centers seek out partners whose research interests them, who have a common mission, and who have skills or technologies they need. Centers are *sought out* by others for their programs, expertise, and data sets, or because of a vaguely articulated sense that the center is "the right place to do this."

The structure of DHC partnerships exists on a spectrum ranging from informal ("handshake agreements") to highly formal (contracts), with a broad array of practices in between. The most informal partnerships generally emerge from personal and professional relationships between the partner and center staff, and proceed solely on the basis of good faith by all parties. Such partnerships are developed through conversations and informal written communications. Partnerships at this level most often occur between the center and faculty, colleagues, and cultural heritage institutions.

The next level of partnership is more formal and includes some type of written agreement. This agreement is a preemptive way to minimize misunderstandings among potential partners, and is not intended as legally binding. Work plans, memoranda of understanding, or requests for proposals are examples of such agreements, and they are used to outline the goals, scope of work, intent, and obligations of the parties. Fellowships are also included here, with the application, guidelines, and fellowship award letters outlining the expectations of both the center and the fellowship recipient. An increasing number of centers are using written agreements for all partnerships, regardless of prior knowledge or relationship with the potential partner.

A special type of partnership exists for those who contribute to online resources created or managed by a center. These partnerships involve membership or contributor agreements that outline specific actions required (e.g., crediting contributions, securing permissions for use of third-party IP) or prohibited (e.g., libelous, defamatory, or obscene behaviors). The agreements are equal parts "social contract" and "rules of the road," emphasizing that contributors are working toward a greater good and outlining expected behaviors. Use of the resource implies consent to the agreement terms, and failure to adhere to these terms results in the member/contributor's having his access rights revoked and/or content contribution deleted. Partnerships at this level generally include members of the educational and academic communities and related professionals groups, as well as the general public (members of which are often invited to contribute to community-based online resources). Although there may be a prior relationship with some of these partners, the numbers are often so large as to preclude such a relationship with all of them.

The most formal level of partnership is a legally binding, contractual relationship. Frequently undertaken with partners in industry, vendors and subcontractors, academic partners in fee-based initiatives, or international organizations, these contracts are vetted at the highest levels of the center or its parent organization. They outline the formalities of the project, as well as legal guarantees such as obligations, fees, warranties, indemnities, and forms of redress. Grant partners are included as a formal level of partnership because the grant process and award enforce formality and conformity with federal, state, or local (e.g., university) requirements. Partnerships that require a contractual relationship involve significant financial interests or technologies, or are international projects that have an inherent complexity born of their international nature.

4.6.2 Unsuccessful Partnerships

Seventy-eight percent of centers reported partnerships that were, in some measure, unsuccessful. Centers were reluctant to describe any of these partnerships as outright failures, characterizing them instead as "difficult" or "less involved" than others. However, they identified many circumstances that can or did lead to unsuccessful partnership experiences, ranging from external factors (e.g., loss of funding) to complex organizational and social issues (e.g., mismatched expectations, lack of institutional support, or staff changes). The following were some of the key issues cited:

Staff Issues
- personality problems (e.g., an overbearing PI) or clashes among staff members
- staff departures, particularly the departure of a PI or a key project "evangelist" whose energy and enthusiasm provided much of the project momentum
- new management that does not have the same vision or motivation as the original management
- a partner liaison who is the wrong person for the job (i.e., lacks the collaborative, hands-on skills required for digital humanities projects)

Partner Lapses or Flaws
- failure to meet obligations or pull their own weight
- insincerity or dishonesty about motives
- an overextended workload that makes it impossible to pay adequate attention to the collaboration
- hoarding intellectual capital; giving nothing away without compensation
- delivering substandard work
- inflexibility
- lack of entrepreneurial experience and an inability to think creatively about the project
- waning interest in the project

Communication Issues
- partner's failure to communicate about why it is not meeting its obligations
- not enough face-to-face meetings, resulting in misunderstandings and mismatched efforts
- leaders agree to things that their staff cannot deliver

Mismatched Expectations
- different perceptions about time and pace of work (e.g., how long it takes to get things done, what "ASAP" means to both partners)
- different expectations about workloads
- disagreements about who is the lead PI and who gets credit for various accomplishments
- misunderstandings about the limits imposed on international partners by their national funding agencies (e.g., an international partner's funds can be used only for students, but the partnership requires professional staff)
- trying to do too much with too few resources

External Factors
- lack of funding options, loss of funding
- project needs exceed current technologies
- project proves uninteresting and not worth pursuing further
- lack of support by the partner's parent institution
- the "price of admission" (e.g., overhead, bureaucratic oversight) proves too high
- lack of time to adequately pursue the project
- language barriers
- cultural distinctions (with international partners)

4.6.3 Elements of a Successful Partnership
Having acquired many years of experience with various partners, DHCs have clear opinions about the characteristics needed to ensure a successful partnership.

Trust as a Baseline Assumption

Partners must operate on the assumption of trust. Ideally, that trust will have been earned from a preexisting relationship between the partners, but even in the absence of such experience, partners must agree to trust one another in order to proceed. Trust must permeate the partnership, so that staff can delegate and conduct work with the knowledge that it will be completed to their satisfaction.

Characteristics of a Good Partner

Partners must have personal attributes that foster trust and collaboration. Creativity, enthusiasm, vigilance, collegiality, competence, and responsibility are highly valued, as are a good reputation, a lack of ego (or the ability to keep it in check), insight into the concerns of others, and transparency in word and deed.

Readiness to Partner

Partners must understand that a DHC partnership is a collaboration. As such, it requires that all parties work on project tasks, support each other and, at times, make allowances for one another. If partners are part of a larger organization, they must garner the support and approval of their parent organization. They must also be capable of working outside their professional boundaries and organizational systems, and bring tangible offerings to the table.

Shared Values

Partners must have the same vision and goals for the project. They must hold a common intellectual stake in the project and in its success.

Available Infrastructure

Partners must have access to physical space. They need stable staffing and good faculty, students, and researchers. The also need appropriate content and technologies to do the job.

Project Preliminaries

Prior to entering a partnership, the parties should conduct a degree of due diligence by looking at their respective performance records and honestly presenting each other with their strengths and weaknesses. As they move closer to partnering, they must identify focused research questions that resonate with all partners. To address these questions concretely, they need a work plan that identifies timetables and budgets, roles and responsibilities, and realistic expectations. Decision-making processes and communication mechanisms must be outlined in advance. All these activities have to be documented, ideally in a written agreement that is signed by all partners and reviewed at regular intervals.

Caring for the Collaboration

A DHC collaboration is often not the central activity of its partners: all parties are involved in other activities, including those that are mission critical to their own organizations. Because of this reality, DHC collaborations must be constantly nurtured and managed. Someone in the partnership must assume the role of a "prodder"— a person who keeps the project moving forward with enthusiasm and constant attention to the project's status and activities. The collaboration's progress must be reviewed frequently to assure that goals remain aligned and that efforts are not straying from the original intent and focus. Regularly scheduled meetings are essential to strengthen personal relationships, defuse tensions, and prevent misunderstandings.

5. Trends and Issues

5.1 Moving toward Maturity

Theorists who study organizations describe their development in terms of life cycle phases such as birth, youth, midlife, and maturity. As organizations move through this life cycle, they become larger, more formal, and more hierarchical. Digital humanities centers, which have now been around for the better part of a decade, are moving from the small, informally run centers that characterized their startup to more organized and structured forms as they head into maturity.

Concomitant with this change is a new set of challenges. Concerns about startup funding and staffing are replaced by concerns about securing sustainable funding and identifying and retaining qualified staff. Initial programs have had time to be tested, and are now being reassessed and reconsidered. Partnerships and collaborations have become the bywords of funding agencies, and digital humanities practitioners and centers are responding in kind. Centers are also embarking on efforts to foster greater communication among one another, both nationally and internationally, as a way of leveraging their numbers for digital humanities advocacy.

In the midst of these changes, centers are assuming a new role, put upon them by humanities departments and universities, as training grounds for digital humanities theory and practice. Academic departments are coming to rely on DHCs to fill gaps in their programs in the area of humanities computing. Universities are calling on DHCs to bring informatics literacy to undergraduate education by incorporating digital humanities into liberal arts curricula. This implicit recognition of the pedagogical value of DHCs in furthering undergraduate and graduate education is helping them leverage their position and status in the university environment.

5.2 Sustainability

Centers continue to struggle over how to sustain their operations in the long term. The classic DHC business model starts with a relatively simple portfolio of funding contributed by a foundation or university, and migrates over time to a complex mix of monies obtained from myriad sources that change yearly because of the short-term nature of grants, state and university budget fluctuations, and an absence of any (or any significant) revenue-generating resources. Increasingly, centers are considering endowments as a way to help bring a greater measure of stability to their ongoing fiscal uncertainties.

Sustainability issues also arise apart from the financial sphere. As the centers mature, many are experiencing the "first-generation" transfer of leadership from the centers' founders. Smooth leadership transitions are directly related to how well the center is positioned financially and politically within its larger infrastructure. Centers that receive little consideration from their parent institution, that have not proven their value to their parent in tangible ways, and that have no governance plan that covers transitions are at great risk of dissolution when current leadership moves on.

Sustainability must also be addressed at the level of DHC projects and products. How can centers sustain projects that have moved from development to implementation and are now in a steady state of production? While some projects (such as pilot projects) do have finite lives, centers increasingly develop resources that are expected by their users to be accessible for the long term. The growing numbers of these types of resources argues for sustainability plans at the project, as well as the center, level.

5.3 Tools

Of all the products DHCs offer, tools have received considerable interest of late within the digital humanities research community. As digital scholarship grows, centers are increasingly taking on a developer's role, creating new tools (or expanding existing ones) to meet their research requirements.

In the interests of furthering research and scholarship, DHC-developed tools are made freely available via various open-source agreements. However, there is some concern that the efforts expended in DHC tool development are not being adequately leveraged across the humanities. A recent study commissioned by CLIR (see Appendix F) found that many of these tools are not easily accessible. They are buried deep within a DHC's Web site, are not highlighted or promoted among the center's products, and lack the most basic descriptions, such as function, intended users, and downloading instructions.

The reason for this state of affairs may be related to how tool development often takes place in DHCs. Centers frequently develop tools within the context of a larger project. Once the project has been completed, the center may become involved in other activities and may not have the resources to address usability issues that would make the tool more accessible for others. The unfortunate result is that significant energy is expended developing a tool that may receive little use beyond a particular center. Funding agencies that support tool development among centers, and that make it a requirement of their grants that the tools be open source, may wish to develop guidelines and provide support for mechanisms that will enhance the usability of existing tools and expose them more prominently to the humanities community. Funding tool development as a piece of a larger center project may not be in the best interest of the humanities community, as individual centers seem unable to maintain these tools beyond the life of the project.

5.4 Preservation

DHCs are aware of the need to preserve the increasing amount of digital materials they produce, but they differ in their perceptions of how to do so. Few centers ascribe to the cardinal rule of digital preservation that preservation processes must be incorporated into the earliest phases (i.e., planning) of the creation of a digital resource. In addition, centers often equate archiving with preservation, not realizing that the former is only one component of a preservation plan.

Some DHCs place the burden of preservation on principal investigators or content providers. This shifting of responsibility is a risky and inadequate solution. Content is only one component that must be preserved in a digital resource. Software functionality, data structures, access guidelines, metadata, and other value-added components to the resource (many of which are created by, and reside within, the centers rather than with the PI or content provider) must also be preserved. Without this "digital ecosystem," the content is stripped of its context and becomes incomprehensible over time.

Preservation is perhaps one of the most urgent problems facing DHCs, as technological changes occur at a breakneck pace and render resources obsolete in only a few years' time. It is likely that older centers already have experienced some loss of resources, and scholars in the near future will be frustrated in their efforts to locate some of the earliest forms of digital scholarship.

5.5 Intellectual Property

The swirl of IP activity under way among DHCs is a response to the growing importance and complexity of the IP arena and the interplay between these issues and the products, services, and activities of the centers. Centers are searching for models that balance their need and desire for openness with a respect for the IP rights of others. Most complain about the "headache" of procuring and managing rights on an individual basis, a time-consuming process that detracts from their research agendas.

Centers also identified new challenges confronting them in the IP arena. A major concern is the IP issues involved in community-built resources. These resources have contributions by potentially thousands of people: traditional rights management does not scale up at this level. Another issue arises with digital art and performance, where the scoring, notating, and rendering needed to display a work creates rights issues at the interface of both copyright and trademark arenas. A third concern pits a user's IP rights against scholarly responsibility for the historical record; namely, how does a center that offers archival or repository services respond to a user's request to remove his or her contribution from the digital resource in the archive? These issues encroach on new terrain that the DHCs feel unprepared to address.

6. DHCs in a Broader Context

6.1 Current Models

An underlying assumption of this study was that centers could be categorized by models of governance (e.g., membership, consortia, independents, university). However, upon closer analysis, this assumption proves difficult to substantiate because of all the exceptions. Two membership-based centers, for example, are governed in whole or in part by a parent university. Some centers still managed by their founders reside in university environments and rely on university resources but apparently operate independently of any overt university governance (oversight is vested in the founders). Another center has strong programmatic and in-kind support from a university, but declares itself "independent" of its governance and oversight.

In sum, governance as a model is too fluid for reliably characterizing the centers in this survey. Funding models also fall short. With one exception (a center funded in its entirety by a single philanthropy), the centers are funded by a diverse and changing mix of support that relies greatly on universities and funding agencies or foundations (see Section 4.5.3).

How, then, can DHCs be categorized? When all the considerations of governance, administration, and operation are considered, the real distinction lies in the focus of the center. The two clear divisions are as follows:

1. Resource focused. Centers are organized around a primary resource, located in a virtual space, that serves a specific group of members. All programs and products flow from the resource, and individual and organizational members help sustain the resource by providing content, and, in some instances, volunteer labor.
2. Center focused. Centers are organized around a physical location, with many diverse projects, programs, and activities that are undertaken by faculty, researchers, and students, and that offer many different resources to diverse audiences. Most of the centers surveyed operate under this model.

HASTAC is an outlier in this discussion. It may be an emerging hybrid between the two models outlined above, in that it pursues diverse projects and programs but is membership based and operates largely in a virtual space.

6.2 Benefits and Limitations of Center- and Resource-Focused Models

The two models that emerge from this analysis have strengths and weaknesses in their respective approaches. Digital humanities centers with a center-based focus can respond quickly and independently to changes in operations and programs because decision making is centralized. These centers are more agile and can experiment and take risks. Their diversified program base means that an unpromising program can be dropped without compromising the center or its other activities. Their physical presence also allows these centers to interact and develop resources with their local communities.

However, the number of activities undertaken by these centers results in a plethora of resources that must be independently maintained and managed. Expertise is dispersed among many projects, to the possible detriment of individual projects. If the center is disbanded, projects without external PI support or a user base willing to sustain the resource risk being orphaned.

Resource-focused centers leverage the knowledge, efforts, and shared interests of their members to create a resource that is beneficial to the entire member community. The resource is built by members who provide content and, in some instances, volunteer services, while the center supports the infrastructure and coordinates, maintains, and makes the resource accessible. Efficiencies exist in areas of content creation and compilation, shared member expertise, and management and sustainability of the resource.

But resource-focused centers also come with compromises. They may not be as agile as other centers and may be more risk averse in their decision making because any change in the operation of the resource directly affects tens of thousands of members. They also may have a hierarchy of member committees or groups that must be contacted before a decision can be made.

In addition, resource-focused centers vest considerable efforts in their startup phase, as they concentrate on compiling a critical mass of content to make the resource valuable and, on front-end systems, accessible. Since the resource is the center's raison d'être, any problems in this early phase can be extremely risky for the center: everything depends on the resource gaining traction.

6.3 Current Models and the Changing Nature of Humanities Scholarship

Both center- and resource-focused models are addressing the changing nature of humanities scholarship by building digital collections and tools to make research more efficient and by exploring different approaches to humanities research. However, some features of these centers may inadvertently hinder wider research and scholarship.

First, the silo-like operation of current centers favors individual projects that are not linked to larger digital resources that would make them more widely known within the research community. When one examines the projects of the 32 surveyed centers en masse, one finds hundreds of projects of potential interest to larger communities that are little known outside the environs of the center and its partners. Moreover, in the absence of preservation plans, many of these projects risk being orphaned over time, as staff, funding, and programming priorities change. In the absence of repositories that enable greater exposure and long-term access, the current landscape of many silo-like centers results in unfettered and untethered digital production that will be detrimental to humanities scholarship.

The silo-like nature of centers also results in overlapping agendas and activities, particularly in areas of training, digitization of collections, and metadata development. With centers competing for the same limited funding pool, they can ill afford to continue with redundant efforts.

The form of collaboration that takes place in today's centers is also inadequate for future scholarship. The differences between the small-scale, narrowly focused collaborations common among DHCs, and the more coordinated, large-scale organizational collaborations characteristic of regional and national centers are more than just differences in size and degree. They involve wholly new processes of management, communication, and interaction.

Of late, a handful of centers are embarking on collaborations that address broader, community-wide issues (such as preserving virtual worlds and strategies for managing born-digital materials). Whether these efforts will move centers toward larger-scale models of collaboration or result in new types of centers is uncertain. However, it is these larger scale efforts, which effectively leverage resources in the community to address broader issues of cyberinfrastructure, that have been missing from the digital humanities scene and that will be necessary to support future humanities research.

6.4 Collaborative Aspects Critical to the Success of Regional or National Centers

As digital humanities computing becomes an integrative, multi-team endeavor, the motivations, support structures, and reward systems that make for successful collaboration become critically important. What aspects of collaboration may be critical to the success of regional or national centers? When the current DHC collaborative landscape is considered in light of successful national collaborations in the scientific community, the following characteristics emerge as particularly important.

Compelling, Community-Wide Research Needs

Digital humanities scholarship thrives on the investigation of research questions both large and small, but it is the former that is the better candidate for regional and national centers. Recent collaborative efforts focusing on digital preservation issues (cited above) offer one example of a "big" problem amenable to a large-scale collaboration. Other compelling research needs might coalesce around cyberinfrastructure that supports digital humanities scholarship, such as sharing advanced computing infrastructure, training in advanced technologies for humanities research, and developing repositories for digital collections.

Larger regional and national efforts may also coalesce around humanities research problems that cut across disciplinary communities. The Pleiades Project, for example, addresses a long-standing need among classicists, archaeologists, historians, literary scholars, and other humanists for a reliable, up-to-date reference for ancient geography. Its large-scale, cross-disciplinary effort may well establish it as a de facto "national" center for the study of ancient geography.

No Center Left Behind

The current (and currently proliferating) landscape is one of individual centers pursuing separate research agendas. These centers have significant professional interests vested in them and considerable amounts of human, financial, and technical infrastructure that is unlikely to be relinquished in deference to other models. Equally important, the centers believe deeply in the value and success of their efforts. Given these circumstances, some DHCs voiced uncertainty about the need for national and regional models, wondering about their purpose, intent, and structure.

Implicit in their concern is the need for clarification of the role of individual DHCs in the context of regional and national centers. Digital humanities centers are a locus of activity that is valued by universities, researchers, faculty, and students. If regional and national models are to be viable, they will need to draw on the individuals and expertise resident in current centers. All parties need greater clarity about the roles for different types of centers (local, regional, and national), as well as strategies for inclusion and interaction among them.

Trust as the Tie that Binds

Academic tenure-and-review committees have long been accused of failing to give credence to digital scholarship. Michael Shanks, codirector of the Stanford Humanities Lab, believes the reason for their hesitation is rooted in trust. These committees want to know if an individual on a team has done the work, or if he or she is simply riding on someone else's coattails.

Shanks (2008) suggests that if collaborative work in the digital humanities moves into what he calls established "laboratories," collaboration will become associated with "continuity, community, and reputation."

> An established lab has a history independent of its members. A track record will establish a reputation that facilitates trust in the collaborative success of the lab—that people there genuinely work together. So when a new joint publication is produced, it will be far easier to associate individual effort and talent with that of the group—individual scholarship gaining credit from its location within a discipline that is precisely identified with its peer practitioners and community.

A shift toward this evaluative framework—one that invests a level of trust in the work of the center and reflects that onto individuals—is needed in the humanities if humanists are to put significant efforts into the collaborative activities of regional and national centers.

Motivations

Acceptance by the academy is important to humanists, but for some collaborations it is not enough to guarantee success. Collaborations involving contributions to a community resource often require other reward systems and incentives to help the resource reach a critical mass and to keep it current and relevant to the community.

The ArchNet project team, for example, found that participant contributions were less than expected several years into the project. They suspect that feedback with their membership (scholars, architects, students, and urban planners interested in Islamic culture) is more critical to participation than realized, and that reward systems that enhance the personal reputation of contributors are important. MERLOT offers such rewards to its contributors by means of a multi-tiered system that includes recognition for exemplary contributions, various service awards, and a peer-review system that rates contributions. Equally important, MERLOT users (higher education faculty and instructors, middle and high school teachers, librarians) offer additional "social rewards": they comment, rate, and incorporate contributions into their personal teaching collections. These activities indicate peer recognition (through use) that enhances a contributor's reputation.

In the sciences, motivating forces take a different form. A study of data contributions to genetics databases revealed that the primary motivation came from two external sources: leading scholarly journals and funding agencies that require data deposition as a prerequisite to publication (for the former) and as a condition of a grant award (for the latter). Altruistic reasons, while less common, were also a source of motivation: contributions were often made out of a sense of obligation to the community or a desire to contribute to a valuable resource.

For national and regional DHCs that emerge around a data resource, identifying motivations and incentives is critical. Some of the more forceful measures (funder-mandated contributions) may have a role, while others (prerequisite for publication) may not. The spirit of sharing and openness that characterizes humanities research must be realistically balanced with professional incentives and opportunities.

The Nature of the Work

Studies on scientific collaborations are abundant, and much of what has been reported mirrors what the centers themselves describe as important characteristics of partnerships (see 4.6.3). However, the traits articulated by DHCs focus on the partner and the process, while studies in the literature also consider how the nature of the work may be related to the success of a collaboration.

A recent study of more than 200 scientific collaboratories suggests that successful large-scale collaborations occur most frequently when the work is easily divided into components rather than "tightly coupled." Even in an age of instantaneous and ubiquitous communication mechanisms, highly integrated projects apparently require the frequent and often innocuous interactions (such as hallway conversations) that occur when collaborators are co-located rather than geographically dispersed.

Studies also show that collaborations organized around the sharing of data or tools are easier to accomplish than are those organized around the sharing of knowledge. Similarly, projects involving aggregation of resources are easier to develop than projects involving co-creation of resources. These findings may be related to the notion about loosely coupled versus tightly coupled projects, but they also likely reflect the belief that it is easier to transmit information than knowledge.

6.5 Some Science Models for Consideration

As part of a large National Science Foundation-funded study of collaboratories, Bos et al. (2007) created a typology of collaboratories based on organizational patterns found in existing large-scale scientific collaborations. Because these authors employed a bottom-up methodology designed to help those who are developing new collaborations, their findings are particularly relevant when considering the types of regional and national centers that might be developed in the humanities.

The classification system developed by Bos and his colleagues is based largely on the goals inherent in existing collaborations. Some of these same collaboratory types already exist in the humanities on a small scale; others are found in community-based projects of interest to the humanities. The classifications defined by Bos et al. are as follows:

- A *Shared Instrument Collaboratory* provides remote access to large, expensive scientific instruments. These types of collaborations are prevalent among astronomers, who need access to large telescopes, and among physicists, who need access to particle accelerators. This model may be relevant for humanists who need access to supercomputers for advanced computational work.
- A *Community Data Systems Collaboratory* is a semipublic (i.e., open to the profession) information resource created, maintained, or enhanced by a geographically distributed community. Well-known biology databases such as the Protein Databank and GenBank are organized as these types of collaborations. In the humanities, the Pleiades Project may be the closest manifestation of this model, although it shares some aspects of the Open Community Contribution System model (below) as well.
- An *Open Community Contribution System* aggregates the efforts of many geographically dispersed individuals toward a common research problem. A project that parallels this model in broad

strokes is the Library of Congress (LC)/Flickr Commons collaboration, in which the collective knowledge of the public is used to enhance cataloging and metadata of LC images via social-networking mechanisms.

- A *Virtual Community of Practice* is a community of individuals who share a research interest and communicate about it online. The community does not undertake joint projects, but it does share professional information, advice, techniques, and contacts. The humanities have many examples of collaborations of this sort, one of the most prominent being H-NET.

- A *Virtual Learning Community* is a community brought together to increase the knowledge of its participants through formal learning programs (not through original research). These communities are often affiliated with degree-granting programs, but they may also be organized around professional development opportunities. For example, a national or regional training center that focused on digital technologies for humanities research would constitute a virtual learning community collaboratory.

- A *Distributed Research Center* is a virtual version of a university research center. This type of collaboratory joins the expertise, resources, and efforts of many individuals interested in a topical area, and conducts joint projects in that area.

- A *Community Infrastructure Project* focuses on developing infrastructure (i.e., tools, protocols, access methods) to further work in a particular domain. The Internet Archive models this type of collaboratory by bringing together efforts of individuals, information science professionals, technologists, and cultural heritage institutions to create an infrastructure for archiving Web and multimedia resources for research.

In looking for collaborative structures that can address the changing needs of humanities scholarship, the models employed by the sciences, which Bos summarizes in the above typology, offer a starting point for discussion. Copious research has been done on these collaborations, particularly on the organizational structures and behaviors that affect their success. As the humanities community considers next steps for the development of digital humanities centers, it might investigate these organizational and social factors more closely and apply their lessons within the context of the humanities.

Appendix A:

Sources for Survey Candidates

Organizations identified as digital humanities centers (or humanities computing centers), or whose names and activities suggest they function as such centers, were gathered from the following resources:

- **The National Endowment for the Humanities Summit of Digital Humanities Centers** (https://apps.lis.uiuc.edu/wiki/download/attachments/21913/DH.Summit.Attendees.pdf?version=1)

  Lists the names of 18 DHCs that participated in this NEH event. Organizations were selected by the Maryland Institute for Technology in the Humanities, a summit organizing partner.

- **The Consortium of Humanities Centers and Institute (CHCI)** http://www.fas.harvard.edu/~chci/index.html

  An international membership organization of more than 150 humanities centers and institutes.

- **Digital Humanities | Center by Type** (http://digitalhumanities.pbwiki.com/centers+by+type.)

  This wiki lists hundreds of organizations worldwide that are involved in humanities computing, including digital libraries, digital humanities projects, and professional associations dedicated to humanities computing. Based on an initial list compiled by Willard McCarty and Matthew Kirschenbaum in 2003, the current wiki is hosted by centerNet, a recently created international network of DHCs.

- **Other**. A handful of organizations were identified from the following resources:
  - DHC Web sites (DHC sites often link to other DHC sites)
  - *Our Cultural Commonwealth: The Report of the American Council of Learned Societies Commission on Cyberinfrastructure for the Humanities and Social Sciences*, 2006 (New York: American Council of Learned Societies)
  - Council on Library and Information Resources
  - Google
  - Wikipedia

Appendix B:

Surveyed Organizations

American Social History Project—Center for Media and Learning
Ancient World Mapping Center
ArchNet
Center for Digital Humanities, University of California, Los Angeles
Center for Digital Research in the Humanities, University of Nebraska
Center for History and New Media, George Mason University
Center for Literary Computing, West Virginia University
Center for New Designs in Learning and Scholarship, Georgetown
　　University
Collaboratory for Research in Computing for Humanities, University
　　of Kentucky
Computer Writing and Research Lab, University of Texas
DXARTS (Digital Arts and Experimental Media)/CARTAH (Center for Ad-
　　vanced Technology in the Arts and Humanities), University of Washington
Experiential Technologies Center (formerly Cultural VR Lab)
Heyman Center for the Humanities, Columbia University
Humanities, Arts, Science and Technology Advanced Collaboratory
　　(HASTAC)
Illinois Center for Computing in Humanities, Arts and Social Science
　　(I-CHASS)
Institute for Advanced Technology in the Humanities (IATH), University of
　　Virginia
Institute for the Future of the Book
Institute for Multimedia Literacy, University of Southern California
Maryland Institute for Technology in the Humanities (MITH)
Matrix—The Center for Humane Arts, Letters and Social Sciences Online
Multimedia Education Resource for Learning and Online Teaching (MERLOT)
National Humanities Center
Perseus Digital Library
Scholarly Technology Group, Brown University
Stanford Humanities Lab
Townsend Center for the Humanities, University of California, Berkeley
University of California Humanities Research Institute
University of Chicago, Division of Humanities, Humanities Computing
Virginia Center for Digital History
Visual Media Center, Columbia University
Women Writers Project
Writing in Digital Environments, Michigan State University

Appendix C:

Survey Instrument

The following template was used to gather information from DHC Web sites and to conduct the phone interviews.

1. General Background Information

Purpose: To gather a basic set of background information about each of the DHCs in the survey.

Information to be collected:
- DHC name and acronym
- Physical and virtual locations
- Year of creation
- Founding history
- Domain (the particular humanities discipline(s) that is a focal point for the DHC, e.g., Islamic architecture, history, gender studies)
- Staffing
- Mission /vision statement; goals and objectives of the DHC
- Brief description of the center
- Constituencies served (e.g., scholars, university community, K–12 teachers, artists)

2. Governance Structure

Purpose: To identify the organizational structure and governance of the DHC, and, if relevant, where the DHC exists within a larger parent organization and how that parent organization oversees the DHC.

Information to be collected:
- Organizational structure (membership, academia, consortium, etc.)
  - Reporting structure (DHC director reports to whom?)
  - Ancillary groups involved in governance and oversight (e.g., advisory committees, steering committees), selection criteria for members of these groups, the duties of these groups, and the terms of service for individuals in these groups

(For DHCs operating under academic/university governance)
- DHC's placement on the university's organizational chart
- If that placement has changed since the DHC's inception, explore why (Was it because of changes in the DHC's circumstances, such as growth, staffing, or cross-campus relationships? Was it the result of changes in the university's circum-

stances, such as institutional restructuring or new management decisions?)

(For DHCs operating under membership governance)
- The DHC's membership base, levels of membership, and benefits associated with each membership level
- Groups that make decisions on behalf of the membership (e.g., board of directors or equivalent); this group's members, affiliations, terms of service, committee appointments, and duties

(For DHCs operating under consortial governance)
- Partners involved in the consortium and their roles and responsibilities
- Groups that make decisions on behalf of the consortium (e.g., board of directors, trustees); this group's members, affiliations, terms of service, and committee appointments and duties
- Formal policies or agreements that govern the consortium
- Distinctions in governance between national/international collaborations

3. Administration

Purpose: To identify how the DHC is organized and administered internally (e.g., Is it a "top-down" management structure, from director to staff?).

Information to be collected:
- Internal organization and reporting structures
- Roles of staff
- Shared academic appointments/arrangements, academic departments involved and the logistics of the shared appointment (percentage of time for each program, shared or distinctive responsibilities, etc.)

4. Operations

Purpose: To identify the programs and activities of each DHC; how the DHC makes decisions about which activities and programs to pursue; to gauge how the DHC allocates time/staffing/funding resources to its activities; and to gauge the extent to which the DHC monitors how (and how much) its products/services are used.

Information to be collected:
- The activities, programs, products, and services offered by the DHC
- How the DHC decides to undertake an activity or program, or offer a product or service (i.e., the decision-making process)
  - Formal or informal processes for decision making
    - How are programs and activities developed, reviewed, funded, documented, and staffed?
    - How does the DHC measure the success of its programs, activities, products, or services?

- Products and services: usage and long-term planning:
  - The volume of use for digital products/services that the DHC offers
  - Characteristics of the user base for the DHC's products and services—who are they, and how are they using the product or service?
  - Plans for preservation and archiving of digital products
  - Intellectual property and ownership concerns related to products and services
- Teaching and other pedagogical activities conducted at or through the center (courses, academic degree programs, internships, fellowships, or other structured educational opportunities)

5. Sustainability

Purpose: To identify resources, efforts undertaken, and plans that allow the DHC to operate for the long term (i.e., the funding, staffing, in-kind agreements for goods/services, business models).

Information to be collected:
- Planning efforts
  - Standard tools (e.g., feasibility studies, needs assessments) used to gauge sustainability prior to the establishment of the DHC
  - Standard tools or methodologies (e.g., strategic plans, business plans) used to plan for the growth and sustainability of the DHC in the long term
- Financial/funding information
  - Sources of funding (general categories [e.g., grants]; and specific funders [e.g., NEH; IMLS])
  - Percentage of funding received from various sources (e.g., 20 percent grants; 15 percent university)
- Business model(s)
  - Current model: Does the DHC believe this model is sustainable?
  - Past models: If the DHC has changed its business model over time, what were the reasons for the change?
- The challenges faced by the DHC that threaten sustainability (e.g., funding, staffing, local institutional/political issues)

6. Partnerships and Collaborations

Purpose: To identify the extent of internal and external partnerships undertaken by DHCs that are not governed under a consortial model and to identify how these partnerships are structured and administered; for all DHCs, to identify why partners are drawn to the center (i.e., reasons for collaborating.)

Information to be collected:
- The DHC's partners (and associated projects)
  - Formal versus informal nature of the partnership
    - If formal, investigate the terms of the partnership (e.g., obligations, expectations, decisions about intellectual property

and ownership)

- National/international nature of partners
- Methods for selecting partners (e.g., Are they solicited by the DHC? Is the DHC approached by interested parties? Both?)
- Whether partnerships emerge from previous relationships between members of the DHC and the partnering organization
- Incentives that encourage people/organizations to partner with the DHC in its various projects
- The DHC's experience with, or ideas about, successful and unsuccessful partnerships

It was assumed that some DHCs would be unable to answer certain questions in the survey, perhaps because they do not track information in certain areas (e.g., user base information) or are not privy to various types of information (e.g., financial data). In the context of this survey, the inability to answer a question was not considered an impediment. In some instances, understanding what an organization did not know about its operations may be a useful indicator of issues that warrant consideration in future discussions of regional or national centers.

Appendix D:

Academic Departments Affiliated with DHCs in This Survey

Architecture and Urban Design
Art History
Cinema Studies
Classics
Comparative Literature
Computer Science and Engineering
Criminology, Law, and Society
Critical Theory
Cultural and Social Anthropology
Dance
Design
Education
Electrical and Computer Engineering
English
French and Italian
History
History of Science and Technology
Interactive Technology and Pedagogy
Modern and Classical Languages
Music
Philosophy
Physics
Rhetoric
Rhetoric and Writing
Speech Communication
Sociology
Spanish and Portuguese
Theology
Writing, Rhetoric, and American Culture

Appendix E:

Bibilography

American Council of Learned Societies. 2006. *Our Cultural Commonwealth: The Final Report of the American Council of Learned Societies Commission on Cyberinfrastructure for the Humanities & Social Sciences.* http://www.acls.org/cyberinfrastructure/OurCulturalCommonwealth.pdf.

Arms, William Y., and Ronald L. Larson. 2007. *The Future of Scholarly Communication: Building Cyberinfrastructure for Cyberscholarship.* Report of a workshop held in Phoenix, AZ, April 17–19, 2007. http://www.sis.pitt.edu/%7Erepwkshop/SIS-NSFReport2.pdf.

Association of Research Libraries. 2006. *To Stand the Test of Time: Long-Term Stewardship of Digital Data Sets in the Science and Engineering.* Report to the National Science Foundation from the ARL Workshop on New Collaborative Relationships: The Role of Academic Libraries in the Digital Data Universe, Arlington, VA, September 26–27, 2006. http://www.arl.org/bm~doc/digdatarpt.pdf.

Beamish, Anne. 2005. Building a Culture of Generosity: Activity, Participation, and Sustainability in an International Design Community. Paper presented at a workshop on Sustaining Community: The Role and Design of Incentive Mechanisms in Online Systems, Sanibel Island, FL, November 6, 2005. http://jellis.org/work/group2005/papers/beamish-group.pdf.

Bement, Arden L. Jr. 2007. Shaping the Cyberinfrastructure Revolution: Designing Cyberinfrastructure for Collaboration and Innovation. *First Monday* 12(6). http://firstmonday.org/issues/issue12_6/bement/index.html.

Bender, Eric. 2004. Rules of the Collaboratory Game. *Technology Review* (November 23). http://www.technologyreview.com/Biztech/13899/.

Berman, Fran. 2004. Cyberinfrastructure and Collaboration. Presentation given at WACE 04 (Workshop on Advanced Collaborative Environments), Nice, France, September 23-24, 2004. PowerPoint presentation available at http://www-unix.mcs.anl.gov/fl/flevents/wace/wace2004/talks/berman.pdf.

Berman, Fran, and Henry Brade. 2005. *Final Report: NSF SBE-CISE Workshop on Cyberinfrastructure and the Social Sciences*. http://vis.sdsc.edu/sbe/reports/SBE-CISE-FINAL.pdf.

BEVO 2008—Building Effective Virtual Organizations. Report of a National Science Foundation Workshop, Washington, DC, January 14–16, 2008. http://www.ci.uchicago.edu/events/VirtOrg2008/.

Bos, Nathan, et al. 2007. From Shared Databases to Communities of Practice: A Taxonomy of Collaboratories. *Journal of Computer-Mediated Communication* 12(2). http://jcmc.indiana.edu/vol12/issue2/bos.html.

Bos, Nathan, Erik Hofer, and Judy Olson. How are public data contributions rewarded in open genetics databases? Paper presented at a Science of Collaboratories Symposium, New Orleans, LA, August 6–12, 2004. PowerPoint presentation available at http://www.scienceofcollaboratories.org/NewsEvents/AOM/Bos_PublicData.ppt.

Burton, Vernon, Simon J. Appleford, and James Onderdonk. 2007. A Question of Centers: One Approach to Establishing a Cyberinfrastructure for the Humanities, Arts, and Social Sciences. *CTWatch Quarterly* 3(2). http://www.ctwatch.org/quarterly/articles/2007/05/a-question-of-centers/.

centerNet. centerNET—*An International Network of Digital Humanities Centers*. http://www.digitalhumanities.org/centernet/.

Choudury, Sayeed. 2007. The Virtual Observatory and the *Roman de la Rose*: Unexpected Relationships and the Collaborative Imperative. *Academic Commons*, special issue on Cyberinfrastructure and the Liberal Arts. http://www.academiccommons.org/commons/essay/VO-and-roman-de-la-rose-collaborative-imperative.

Crane, Greg. 2003. Culture and Cyberinfrastructure: The Need for a Cultural Informatics. Paper presented at the National Science Foundation Post-Digital Library Futures Workshop, Cape Cod Chatham, MA, June 15–17, 2003. http://www.sis.pitt.edu/~dlwkshop/paper_crane.html.

Crane, Greg. 2007. Open Access and Institutional Repositories: The Future of Scholarly Communications. *Academic Commons*, special issue on Cyberinfrastructure and the Liberal Arts. http://www.academiccommons.org/commons/review/gregory-crane.

CREW—Collaboratory for Research on Electronic Work. http://www.crew.umich.edu/.

Davidson, Cathy, and David Theo Goldberg. 2007. *The Future of Learning Institutions in a Digital Age*—About This Project. http://www.futureofthebook.org/HASTAC/learningreport/about.

Green, David. 2007. Cyberinfrastructure For Us All: An Introduction to Cyberinfrastructure and the Liberal Arts. *Academic Commons*, special issue on Cyberinfrastructure and the Liberal Arts. http:// www.academiccommons.org/commons/essay/cyberinfrastructure-introduction.

Jackson, Steven J., Paul N. Edwards, Geoffrey C. Bowker, and Cory P. Knobel. June 2007. Understanding Infrastructure: History, Heuristics, and Cyberinfrastructure Policy. *First Monday* 12(6). http://firstmonday.org/issues/issue12_6/jackson/index.html.

Kahin, Brian, and Steven J. Jackson. June 2007. Preface. Cyberinfrastructure Comes of Age? *First Monday* 12(6). http://www.firstmonday.org/issues/issue12_6/index.html.

Lawrence, Katherine A., Thomas A. Finholt, and Il-hwan Kim. 2007. Warm Fronts and High Pressure Systems: Overcoming Geographic Dispersion in a Meteorological Cyberinfrastructure Project. CREW Technical Report Number CREW-07-08. http://www.crew.umich.edu/publications/tr_07_08.html.

Lesk, Michael. 2007. From Data to Wisdom: Humanities Research and Online Content. *Academic Commons*, special issue on Cyberinfrastructure and the Liberal Arts. http://www.academiccommons.org/commons/essay/michael-lesk.

Mackie, Christopher J. 2007. Cyberinfrastructure, Institutions, and Sustainability. *First Monday* 12(6). http://www.firstmonday.org/issues/issue12_6/mackie/index.html.

McNamara, Carter. 2007. Basic Overview of Organizational Life Cycles. http://www.managementhelp.org/org_thry/org_cycl.htm.

Myers, Jim. 2008. Cyberinfrastructure Lessons. Presentation at BEVO 2008: Building Effective Virtual Organizations, an NSF Workshop, Washington, DC, January 14-16, 2008. PowerPoint presentation at http://www.ci.uchicago.edu/events/VirtOrg2008/files/CyberinfrastructureLessons.pdf.

National Science Foundation. 2007. *Cyberinfrastructure Vision for 21st Century Discovery*. http://www.nsf.gov/pubs/2007/nsf0728/index.jsp.

National Science Foundation. 2003. *Report of the National Science Foundation Blue-Ribbon Advisory Panel on Cyberinfrastructure*. http://www.nsf.gov/od/oci/reports/toc.jsp.

Nichols, Stephen. 2007. Digital Scholarship: What's All the Fuss? *CLIR Issues 58*. http://www.clir.org/pubs/issues/issues58.html#digital.

Olson, Judith S., Gary M. Olson, and Erik C. Hofer. 2005. What Makes for Success in Science and Engineering Collaboratories? Proceedings of the Workshop on Advanced Collaborative Environments, Redmond, WA, September 8-9, 2005. http://www-unix.mcs.anl. gov/fl/flevents/wace/wace2005/papers/olson.pdf.

Resources: Collaboratories at a Glance. http://www.scienceofcollaboratories.org/Resources/colisting.php.

Scholarly Communication Institute | Current Institute. http://www.uvasci.org/current-institute/.

Science of Collaboratories Home. http://www.scienceofcollaboratories.org/.

Shanks, Michael. 2008. The Idea of a Humanities Lab. *Weblog: Michael Shanks - Archaeologist*. http://documents.stanford.edu/Michael-Shanks/218.

SPARC: Background. Space Physics and Aeronomy Research Collaboratory (SPARC). http://www.si.umich.edu/sparc/background. htm.

Spencer, B., R. Butler, K. Ricker, D. Marcusiu, T. Finholt, I. Foster, and C. Kesselman. 2006. Cyberenvironment Project Management: Lessons Learned. http://neesgrid.ncsa.uiuc.edu/documents/CP-MLL.pdf.

Unsworth, John. 2007. Digital Humanities Centers as Cyberinfrastructure. Paper presented at the Digital Humanities Centers Summit, National Endowment for the Humanities, Washington, DC, April 12, 2007. http://www3.isrl.uiuc.edu/~unsworth/dhcs.html.

Waters, Donald. 2003. Beyond Digital Libraries: The Organizational Design of a New Cyberinfrastructure. Paper presented at the National Science Foundation Post-Digital Library Futures Workshop, Cape Cod Chatham, MA, June 15–17, 2003. http://www2.sis.pitt. edu/~dlwkshop/paper_waters.html.

Using New Technologies to Explore Cultural Heritage. Conference sponsored jointly by the National Endowment for the Humanities and the Consiglio Nazionale delle Richerche of Italy, Washington, DC, October 5, 2007. http://www.neh.gov/DigitalHumanities/Conference_07Oct/DH_Conference.html.

Zafrin, Vika. 2006. The Virtual Humanities Lab and the Evolution of Remote Collaboration. Podcast of presentation given at the Maryland Institute for Technology in the Humanities, University of Maryland at College Park, MD, November 7, 2006. http://khelone.umd.edu/staff/dreside/dd-11-7-06.mp3.

Appendix F:

Tools for Humanists

Tools for Humanists Project
Final Report
April 18, 2008

Council on Library and Information Resources
Lilly Nguyen and Katie Shilton

Contents

1. Introduction—Why Tools?

Digital tools are an important component of the cyberinfrastructure that supports digital humanities research (UVA 2005). Tools for humanities research—software or computing products developed to provide access, interpret, create, or communicate digital resources—are increasingly developed and supported by Digital Humanities Centers (DHCs) and the wider digital humanities community. Such tools represent a significant investment of research and development time, energy, and resources.

Tools are distinct from other assets developed and cultivated by DHCs. These additional assets include *resources* and *collections*. Researchers use tools to access, manipulate, or interpret resources or collections, while resources are "data, documents, collections, or services that meet some data or information need" (Borgman 2007). In a recent report on cyberinfrastructure for the humanities and social sciences, the American Council of Learned Societies (2006) distinguished tools from collections by emphasizing that tool building is dependent on the existence of collections. Resources or collections may be associated with a tool and may serve as an indicator of a tool's functionality and value, but are not themselves tools. As such, we define tools as software developed for the creation, interpretation, or sharing and communication of digital humanities resources and collections.

Because tools provide the action (rather than the subject) of digital humanities research, digital tools are one of the most extensible assets within the digital humanities community. Researchers can share tools to perform diverse and groundbreaking research, making them a critical part of the digital humanities cyberinfrastructure. If these tools are not visible, accessible, or understandable to interested researchers, they become less likely to be used broadly, less able to be built upon or extended, and therefore less able to support and broaden the research for which they are intended. CLIR's interest in supporting the cyberinfrastructure of digital humanities has spurred us to evaluate the landscape of digital tools available for humanities research.

2. Research Questions

CLIR's concern for accessibility and clarity of tools is based on a larger study of the characteristics of digital humanities centers that frequently make their tools available to researchers. This context prompted the two research questions that guide this evaluation project.

RQ1: How easy is it to access DHC tools?

RQ2: How clear are the intentions and functions of DHC tools?

The evaluation research outlined in this report answers these questions by delineating variables that respond to the goals of accessibility and clarity. We use these variables to evaluate a purposive sample of 39 digital humanities tools.

3. Methodology

Following a scope of work provided by CLIR, this evaluation project focused on defining elements that contribute to findable, usable digital tools and on ranking existing DHC tools according to these elements. Our first challenge was to clarify the definition of *digital tool* through a literature review on cyberinfrastructure and digital humanities. This allowed us to refine and define distinct characteristics of digital tools and to delineate a sample set of tools hosted by the DHCs listed in Appendix B (page 48). Section 3.a. details this first phase of the evaluation research.

Once we had determined our sample, the next step was to create an evaluation framework and instrument. Concentrating on CLIR's evaluation interests of findability and usability, we surveyed our sample of 39 tools and looked for elements that made tools easy to access and understand. We describe the process of creating an evaluation framework in Section 3.b.

After drafting our sample set and scales, we submitted an evaluation strategy to CLIR for approval. We then performed several trial evaluations to check for interindexer consistency. This is detailed in Section 3.b.iii. After several iterations of this consistency check, we divided the 39 tools in half, and each researcher evaluated her assigned tools. We then combined our data and began the data analysis, described in Section 4.

3.a. Definitions, Sample, Limitations, and Assumptions

3.a.i. Definitions

We defined tools for humanists as software intended to provide access to, create, interpret, or share and communicate digital humanities resources. Further, the tools evaluated in this project are products of the digital humanities community and are designed to be *extensible*, that is, used with resources beyond those provided by the creating institution. We grounded this definition within a typology of digital tools drawn from the wider digital humanities literature. Our typology defines tools according to three dimensions: *objectives*, *technological origins*, and *associated resources*.

Tools as defined by objectives

Based on digital humanities literature, researchers use digital tools for the following objectives:

- *access and exploration of resources*: to make specialized content "intellectually as well as physically accessible" (Crane et al. 2007); and
- *insight and interpretation*: to enable the user to find patterns of significance and to interpret those patterns (ACLS 2006).

In addition, based on our observation of DHCs in the United States, we propose additional tool objectives:

- *creation*: to make new digital objects or digital publications from humanities resources; and
- *community and communication*: to share resources or knowledge.

These four objectives guided the selection of our sample tools from the DHC sites identified by Diane Zorich's work. These objectives suggest future evaluations of tools that extend beyond accessibility and clarity to evaluate how well DHC tools support and facilitate these critical functions. Given CLIR's interest in questions relating to the clarity of and access to tools, we have not yet explored the use, value, or effectiveness of tools according to these objectives. That is to say, we did not consider issues of performance, which is a promising area for future consideration.

Tools as defined by site of technological origin

On the basis of our observation of DHC Web sites, we found variation in communities of tool authorship. Some tools were the product of a single center (e.g., the Berlin Temporal Topographies built by Stanford Humanities Lab). Some tools started outside of the humanities community, but centers or cooperatives adapted the tools heavily for humanities research (e.g., SyllabusFinder adapted from the Google search engine by George Mason University's [GMU's] Center for History and New Media). Some tools were developed outside of the humanities community and appropriated, with little or no modification, by the humanities community (e.g., blogs or wikis). The spectrum of technological origins thus spanned a range from single-center authorship to appropriation from an outside community (see Table 1). We considered only tools authored by a single institution in the digital humanities community or by a collaboration of institutions in the digital humanities community for our final sample group.

Tools as defined by associated resources

Our observation of DHC Web sites also illustrated that tools vary along a spectrum according to the resources with which they interact. Some tools work only with resources provided by the center (e.g., the Women's Studies Database at the Maryland Institute for Technology in the Humanities). Other tools can interact with resources provided by the center in addition to outside resources (e.g., BATS assistive technology created by the Ancient World Mapping Center). Finally, some tools work exclusively with outside resources, and centers provide no in-house collections for use with the tool (e.g., the Center for History and New Media's Omeka digital display tool). For our study, we focused on tools that interact (1) with resources provided by the center and outside resources, and (2) with outside resources only.

We excluded tools that interact only with in-house resources from our sample based on the view that extensible tools are most useful for researchers, as they allow individuals to explore or analyze their own data and resources. As previously explained, we judged extensible tools to be of the most interest to the broader infrastructure for the digital humanities, as such tools enable broad community use as well as highly customizable, individualized research.

3.a.ii. Evaluation Sample

Given the limitation to extensible tools, we chose to confine our survey of DHC tools to items created by or adapted within the humanities community that were designed for use with outside resources or a mix of outside and indigenous resources. We excluded those tools that had been developed in the outside (nondigital humanities) community or that had been developed to function with only a single collection or resource. This allowed us to narrow our sample to 39 tools for evaluation. Table 1 illustrates how the 39 tools group according to two variables: (1) technological development (developed by a DHC or a humanities community); and (2) associated resources (usable with outside resources or mixed resources).

3.a.iii. Research Limits and Assumptions

This evaluation of tools created by DHCs is part of a much larger CLIR survey of the landscape of DHCs that determined certain features of our study. That survey predetermined the population of centers from which we drew our sample. We identified tools from each of these centers. We excluded certain parameters that we might have considered in defining the scope. Specifically, we did not employ user population as means of selecting the sample of tools to study, and we used a limited understanding of the idea of "findability."

Based on the literature, we assumed that a wide swath of faculty, independent researchers, university staff, and graduate and undergraduate students utilize humanities cyberinfrastructure (ACLS 2006). Findability bears heavily on questions of accessibility of digital tools and suggests users' ability to search and find tools without previous knowledge of the tools. As such, findability would consider a wider breadth of information-seeking technologies, including search engines, and would reflect the highly complicated—and more realistic—landscape that users encounter when trying to search and find digital humanities tools. In order to limit our evaluation to dimensions of accessibility and clarity of intention/function within the context of the given DHC settings, we did not evaluate findability of digital tools. We excluded findability in a general sense and focused solely on questions of tool accessibility within these sites. Findability depends upon the metadata associated with tools, as well as on the structure of the system supporting the Web sites that provide the first point of access for users, since Web crawlers (and hence indexing) may go only two or three levels into a site. Thus, evaluating the existing search engines, systems, and metadata structures and standards associated with tools would be valuable follow-up research. Given the limits and needs of CLIR's research directive, however, findability from outside the Web site was beyond the scope of this project.

We have also made some basic assumptions about users. In order to evaluate accessibility that excludes findability, we assumed users who already know that tools are available, and who know to explore DHC Web sites for tools. We evaluated whether such a user can easily find the tool on a DHC's Web site, easily understand the tool's intention, and easily begin using the tool.

Table 1: Matrix of Tools for Evaluation (Final Sample Group)

	Digital Humanities Center	**Humanities Community** (also if DHCs partner w/other organizations)
OUTSIDE RESOURCES	Collaborative Genealogy—Jenkins Collab.	Video Annotation System (HASTAC and Duke)
	Collaborative Timeline—Jenkins Collab.	HASS Grid Portal (HASTAC and UCHRI)
	Combinformation, Texas A&M	Historinet and ADAA (Advanced Digital Archive Assistance)—HASTAC and Stanford Humanities Lab
	CommentPress—Institute for the Future of the Book	Syllabus Finder, GMU
	CUSeeMe Reflector, WVU	
	Digital Discernment, Georgetown	
	Edition Production Technology (EPT), ARCHway Project	
	English to Greek Word Search—Perseus	
	English to Latin Word Search—Perseus	
	Greek Morphological Analysis—Perseus	
	Interactive Archaeological Knowledge System—Matrix	
	Latin Morphological Analysis—Perseus	
	Media Matrix—Matrix	
	Omeka, GMU	
	Poll Builder, GMU	
	Project Pad—Matrix	
	Scholar Press, GMU	
	Scribe, GMU	
	SOPHIE—Institute for the Future of the Book	
	Survey Builder, GMU	
	Tech Ticker—Jenkins Collab.	
	The Poster Tool, Georgetown	
	Virtual Lightbox—MITH	
	Web Scrapbook, GMU	
	Zotero, GMU	
MIXED RESOURCES	BATS, Ancient World Mapping Center	CITRIS Collaborative Gallery Builder, HASTAC
	DySE Generator, UCLA	
	Grassroots—WIDE MSU	
	History Engine—Virginia Center for Digital History	
	Ink—WIDE MSU	
	Literacy Resource Exchange—WIDE MSU	
	Token X, University of Nebraska	
	Virtual Humanities Lab—STG Brown	
	vrNav, UCLA	

Another assumption made early in our work, and one that has not proved entirely tenable, is that tools could be downloaded. Such tools are easy to envision. They are discrete pieces of software run on a user's own computer and resources. However, a focus on software download is increasingly irrelevant in an era when both storage and computing power are moving into the "cloud" (i.e., the combined computing power of servers owned by others) (Borgman 2007). We therefore evaluated tools that can be downloaded (e.g., UCLA's Experimental Technologies Center's vrNav virtual reality software) as well as tools used online and supported by the servers of others (i.e., the University of Nebraska Center for Digital Research in the Humanities' Token X text-visualization tool). We also considered the clarity of the process of using tools with data sets or resources–either on a user's computer or in the cloud—when evaluating the usability of these tools.

3.b. Evaluation Framework and Instrument

We designed this evaluation framework to answer our research questions:
• How easy is it to access DHC tools?
• How clear are the intentions and functions of DHC tools?

Based on these questions, we created two scales:
• Ease of Access: Discovering Tools
• Clarity of Use: Enabling Use of Tools

To address these research questions, we developed scales to measure the strength of each of the 39 tools with regard to four variables: (1) identification of tool; (2) feature, display, and access; (3) clarity of description; and (4) clarity of operation. To construct measurable scales, we divided the variables into distinct indicators that we could rank as poor, moderate, or excellent. The next sections describe the indicators and variables. We conclude the evaluation framework with a table that provides details on the entire evaluative schema.

3.b.i. Ease of Access: Discovering Tools

This scale includes variables that represent the process of discovering available tools. Discovering and accessing available tools includes variables such as:
• ways in which DHCs *identify* tools to users (in terms of language and word choice and visibility on the page); and
• how DHCs *feature*, *display*, and *provide access* to tools on their Web sites through placement within the Web site and access to downloading the tool or uploading data.*
  See Table 2.

---

* Exporting the results of data-tool interaction did not seem to be an emphasis in the tools we examined. (For example, tools such as Token X allow users to play with their data on the tool's site, but without possibility of exporting altered data. However, uploading data is not always a question of uploading data to a tool site. Several tools allow users to download the tool, and then upload data to the tool, but everything stays on a user's computer. This shows that there are many possible permutations of downloading, uploading, local, and cloud computing.

Table 2: Ease-of-Access Scale

Variable	Component	Poor	Moderate	Excellent
Identification of tools	Word choice	Use of broader term	Use of narrower term	Use of the term tool
	Visibility on page	Buried within body of text	Moderately visible	Highly visible
Feature, Display, and Access	Tool placement within Web site	Buried under multiple pages (clicks)	2 clicks	1 click
	Downloading	Download link separated from tool description		Download link embedded in tool description
	Uploading	Link to upload dataset/resources separated from tool description		Link to upload dataset/resources embedded in tool description

3.b.ii. Clarity of Use—Enabling the Use of Tools

We also evaluated the 39 tools on a scale representing the clarity of the intentions and functions of the tool. This scale depends upon variables that represent the process of interacting with a tool after discovery. Clarity of use variables include:

Clarity of tool description: Are the tool's functions and target user group clearly and concisely stated? Clear and concise descriptions enable and encourage individuals to use and download the tools.

Clarity of tool operation: Can the tool be previewed? Can most users operate the tool on their systems? Is it clear how users can import or upload their datasets or resources for use with the tool?

See Table 3.

3.b.iii. Interindexer Consistency

To assure interindexer consistency, we selected two tools and each researcher (Katie and Lilly) coded the tools independently. After coding, the researchers compared scores. Interindexer consistency after the first evaluation was only 32 percent. To improve consistency, the researchers identified the points of divergence and discussed why they had coded the tools differently. Each researcher explained her justification and definitions. Together, the researchers created a granular, detailed definition of each variable to fully standardize the evaluation metrics (see Appendix F-2 for the granular scale definitions). After two more rounds of evaluation and discussion, during which the researchers each coded a total of seven tools, interindexer consistency reached 100 percent.

Table 3: Clarity-of-Use Scale

Variable	Component	Poor	Moderate	Excellent
Clarity of description	Function	Function of tool not stated	Function of tool difficult to understand	Function of tool stated in an easy to understand manner
	User group	Intended user groups not stated	User group difficult to understand	Intended user groups clearly stated (by subject, age, discipline, etc.)
Clarity of operation	Preview	Tool cannot be previewed	Tool can be previewed via screenshots	Tool can be previewed via demonstrations
	Technical requirements	Operating system requirements/limitations not provided	Operating system requirements/limitations are murky, hard to find, buried on page	Clear and concise operating system requirements/ limitations provided
	Technical requirements —additional software	The tool requires additional software; however, it does not provide clear statements about these requirements and does not provide direct links to the additional software or instructions on accessing and installing	[any 2 out of these 3] Clear descriptions on additional requirements Direct links to additional software Instructions on accessing and installing software	The tool does not require any additional software to run -or- The DHC provides clear statements on additional requirements, while providing direct links AND instructions on accessing and installing additional software requirements
	Instructions for download	No instructions are provided on how to download a tool	Instructions are either difficult to understand or not readily accessible	Clear and easy-to-understand instructions on how to download the tool are provided and readily accessible
	Instructions for data import or upload	No instructions are provided on how to connect data or resources to a tool	Instructions are either difficult to understand or not readily accessible	Clear and easy to understand instructions are provided and readily accessible

4. Results and Observations

To organize data collection surrounding the variables previously discussed, above, we applied the following data collection instrument to each of the 39 tools. For each variable, we gave tools a numerical score based on the definitions below:

Table 4: Variables Scales

25 Variables Total	**POINTS:**	**0**	**1**	**2**	**3**	**4**
IDENTIFICATION						
1a	Word Choice	Not identified	Broader Term	Narrower Term	Tool	
1b	Visibility	N/A	Buried	List	Featured	
FEATURE AND DISPLAY						
2a	Tool placement on site		Buried	2 click	1 click	
2b	Downloading (1) - Available	No	Yes			
2c	Downloading (2) - Where		Elsewhere	Resources Page	Tool Page	
2d	Uploading (1)	No	Yes			
2e	Uploading (2)		Elsewhere	Resources Page	Tool Page	
CLARITY OF DESCRIPTION						
3a	Function (1) - Stated	No	Yes			
3b	Function (2) - Clear	No	Yes			
3c	Function (3) - Concise	No	Yes			
3d	User group (1) - Stated	No	Yes			
3e	User group (2) - Clear	No	Yes			
3f	User group (3) - Concise	No	Yes			
CLARITY OF OPERATION						
4a	Preview (1) - Available	No	Yes			
4b	Preview (2) - What type	Other (list)	Screenshots	Movies	Demo	All
4c	Support Provided	None	Email	Forums	Tutorial	
4d	Technical Requirements (1) - Stated	No	Yes			
4e	Technical Requirements (2) - Notification of additional software required	No	Yes			
4f	Technical Requirements (3) - Software links provided	No	Yes			
4g	Technical Requirements (4) - OS	None	1 OS	2 or more OS		
4h	Instructions for Download (1) - Stated	No	Yes			
4i	Instructions for Download (2) - Clear	No	Yes			
4j	Instructions for Download (3) - Concise	No	Yes			
4k	Instructions for Data Interaction (1) - Stated	No	Yes			
4l	Instructions for Data Interaction (2) - Clear	No	Yes			
4m	Instructions for Data Interaction (3) - Concise	No	Yes			

Scores for the 39 tools ranged from 33 points to 6 points. We calculated the mean and standard deviation for the tools' total scores ($x = 17$, $sd = 7$). We then used the standard deviation to analyze the overall distribution of the tools and identify how tool groups would be constructed.

- Tools scoring 24 points or above were categorized within the highest-scoring group.
- Those scoring between 10 and 23 points were placed within the middle-scoring set.
- Those scoring 9 points or less were categorized within the lowest-scoring group.

The highest-scoring group comprised 7 tools, the middle group 24 tools, and the bottom group 8 tools. Organizing the tools into three sets allowed us to average individual variable scores within each set. This enabled us to compare the major differences among the groups. Table 5 shows which tools fell within each of the groups.

Table 5: Highest, Lowest, and Middle Tool Groups

Highest Group	Score
Zotero	33
Omeka	30
Sophie	28
Token X	27
Scribe	25
Virtual Lightbox	25
Digital Discernment	24

Lowest Group	Score
CITRUS Collaboratory Gallery Builder	9
Ink	8
Edition Production Technology	7
DySE Generator	7
Video Annotation System	7
Historinet	6
Hass Grid Portal	6
Poster Tool	6

Middle Group	Score
Virtual Humanities Lab	23
Combinformation	22
BATS	21
ScholarPress	21
CommentPress	20
Web Scrapbook	20
Survey Builder	20
Syllabus Finder	19
Media Matrix	19
Collaborative Genealogy	19
Project Pad	18
History Engine	18
Grassroots	18
Poll Builder	17
vrNav	17
Literacy Resource Exchange	16
Tech Ticker	16
English to Greek Word Search	15
Interactive Archeology Knowledge System	14
Collaborative Timeline	14
CUSeeMe Reflector	11
English to Latin Word Search	10
Greek Morphology Analysis	10
Latin Morphology Analysis	10

4.a. Ease of Access

Feature and display: *Word choice* was a major distinguisher of highest-rated tools. Highest-rated tools tended to use the specific word "tool" to distinguish a tool, rather than a general term such as "project" or "resource." *Tool placement on site* was another distinguishing feature. Highest-scoring tools were often one click away from the DHC's home page; bottom tools were two or more clicks away. *Visibility* of the tools was universally mediocre. Most DHCs included tools in long lists of projects or resources; only a few DHCs featured tools prominently or separately.

Most tools were available for download or equipped to allow upload of users' data. A few tools allowed for both. However, among those tools that did provide download or upload capability, *findability of downloading or uploading* set the highest-scoring tools apart. The lowest-ranking tools suffered from difficult-to-find downloading or upload modalities. In a few cases, downloading or uploading was not available even for tools that had been under development for several years.

4.b. Clarity of Use

Clarity of description: While most tools stated their function, *clarity and conciseness of the functions* set highest-ranking tools apart from lower-rated tools. Similarly, *clarity and conciseness of user group statement* separated tools. While most tools stated a user group, the clarity and conciseness of that statement set top-rated tools apart. Tools in the highest-scoring group typically provided clear and concise descriptions of user groups that made it easy to infer who would most benefit from using the tool. Most tools stated their function in some form, although few of these definitions were clear or concise. Only three tools did not state their function at all. A slim majority of tools stated their user group in some form. Sixteen out of thirty-five tools did not state a user group.

Clarity of operation: *Availability and type of preview* was another distinguishing factor. Highest-scoring tools not only made previews available but used sophisticated interactive previews such as demos, rather than static forms such as screenshots. Highest-scoring tools offered support in the form of tutorials, forums, and FAQs, in addition to providing e-mail support. The highest-rated tools also clearly stated technical requirements for using the tool and provided links to any required additional software. Additionally, tools in the top group were more likely to provide cross-platform usability, supporting more than one operating system. Perhaps the most glaring problem was the universal weakness of clarity and conciseness of download instructions or data interaction instructions: 29 of 39 tools offered no instructions for download; 22 of 39 offered no instructions for data interaction.

Table 6 provides a breakdown of all the variables among the three tool groups.

Table 6: Ranked Average Score Breakdown

		Top Average	Middle Average	Bottom Average
IDENTIFICATION				
1a	Word Choice	1.9	1.4	0.9
1b	Visibility	1.7	1.6	1.6
FEATURE AND DISPLAY				
2a	Tool placement on site	2.1	1.5	1.3
2b	Downloading (1) - Available	0.9	0.3	0.0
2c	Downloading (2) - Where	2.3	0.9	0.0
2d	Uploading (1)	0.9	0.5	0.0
2e	Uploading (2)	1.4	0.9	0.0
CLARITY OF DESCRIPTION				
3a	Function (1) - Stated	1.0	0.9	1.0
3b	Function (2) - Clear	1.0	0.7	0.4
3c	Function (3) - Concise	1.0	0.7	0.6
3d	User group (1) - Stated	0.7	0.6	0.5
3e	User group (2) - Clear	0.6	0.3	0.3
3f	User group (3) - Concise	0.6	0.3	0.3
CLARITY OF OPERATION				
4a	Preview (1) - Available	0.9	0.8	0.1
4b	Preview (2) - What type	2.4	1.7	0.1
4c	Support Provided	1.9	1.1	0.0
4d	Technical Requirements (1) - Stated	0.7	0.4	0.0
4e	Technical Requirements (2) - Notification of additional software required	0.7	0.4	0.0
4f	Technical Requirements (3) - Software links provided	0.7	0.2	0.0
4g	Technical Requirements (4) - OS	1.6	0.4	0.0
4h	Instructions for Download (1) - Stated	0.7	0.2	0.0
4i	Instructions for Download (2) - Clear	0.3	0.1	0.0
4j	Instructions for Download (3) - Concise	0.3	0.1	0.0
4k	Instructions for Data Interaction (1) - Stated	0.7	0.5	0.0
4l	Instructions for Data Interaction (2) - Clear	0.3	0.4	0.0
4m	Instructions for Data Interaction (3) - Concise	0.3	0.3	0.0

4.c. Discussion

Overall, the 39 tools surveyed here performed better on variables measuring ease of access than on variables measuring clarity of use. Most of the DHC sites provided adequate-to-excellent access to tools through appropriate word choices that aid users in identifying tools, and tool placement within the design of the DHC home page that allows users to discover tools while browsing.

However, access to these tools was often impeded by low visibility of, and obscured access to, downloading and uploading features. Clarity of use was a widely problematic dimension of existing tools. Statements summarizing the basic functionality of a tool appeared to be the most frequent technique employed by tool developers to clarify tool use. However, the highest-scoring tools also supplemented these descriptions with (1) detailed statements documenting technical requirements for tool use; (2) sophisticated previews to allow users a sense of the look, feel, and interaction with the tool; and (3) additional support for users in the forms of tutorials, FAQs, manuals, or forums.

We noticed a few problems not captured in our variable scale, but worth mentioning. As we progressed through our evaluation, we came across the phenomenon of *orphan tools*—tools that are operational but not linked to or referred to by their DHC in any way. MSU's Media Matrix and four translation tools authored by the Perseus project (five tools total) are not linked from their DHC sponsor's Web sites.

A number of tools do not feature download or upload capabilities because they are not ready for public consumption. For newer tools (such as MSU's Interactive Archeological Knowledge System), this is understandable, but some of these tools seem to have been under development for quite some time. Tools such as CITRIS Collaborative Gallery Builder, HASTAC's Video Annotation System, MSU's Ink, and Stanford Humanities Lab's Historinet are not ready for public use though they have been under development for several years.

Finally, we noticed a number of tools that appear to have been abandoned by their creators. Often the code is available for other developers to work on, but there is no further development occurring at the DHC. Examples include the Ancient World Mapping Center's BATS, Matrix's Project Pad, and STG Brown's Virtual Humanities Lab.

5. Recommendations

On the basis of this evaluation, we offer the following recommended best practices for tool design for humanities scholars.

(1) **Feature tools**. Highlighting your tools using Web design and language draws desired users to the software that a DHC has spent time and effort developing. Best practices for featuring tools include using appropriate word choices. A specific term like *tool* allows users to find and use relevant software more quickly. Another important measure is featuring the tool on the DHC's Web site using design techniques, rather than burying it in a bulleted list of projects or resources.

(2) **Clarify the tool's purpose and audience**. Users investigating a tool need to know both the intended function of the tool and whether the tool is appropriate for their uses. Clear, concise information about your tool's purpose and audience will help users make this decision.

(3) **Make previews available**. The more a user can find out about a tool in advance of downloading or uploading the data, the better. Screenshots, tutorials, and demos can provide users with helpful information regarding the look and feel of your tool.

(4) **Provide support**. Including an e-mail address for users who have questions is a start, but FAQs and searchable forums are also valuable aids to clarity and successful tool operation.

(5) **State technical requirements**. Users need to know whether they can download or use a tool with their current technology. State and provide links to any additional software needed to help users make this determination. If your tool needs nothing but a Web browser, say so! Enable use through clear requirements.

(6) **Provide clear, easy instructions for download or data interaction**. This critical step for clarity of tool use was almost universally lacking in our sample. Without directions, users will have trouble installing your tool, or uploading their data for use with your tool.

(7) **Plan for sustainability**. Making the tool available after a grant period has run out is a major challenge. During tool creation, plan for how you will make it available to users—and even iterated and improved—after the development period has ended.

6. Lessons Learned and Implications for Future Research

From the beginning of this project, the term *tool* proved slippery and problematic. Digital humanities center sites featured projects, resources, software, and occasionally tools, but it was difficult to determine the parameters that lead to identification of a tool. This led to a lengthy definition-building process at the beginning of this research. We hope the elements of a tool that we have delineated (objectives, site of development, and associated resources) will introduce precision and enable greater rigor in subsequent research.

This research had several limitations that we recommend be addressed in future projects. Given the scope of the larger project within which this evaluation was embedded, we considered only identification, features, and display of a tool *within* a DHC site in the notion of findability. This view disregards tool findability from outside of the centers via search engines, browsing, etc., that may more accurately reflect everyday user scenarios. This broader concept of findability bears on several structural issues, including search engine functionality, metadata associated with tools, and DHC site structure. The implications of a broader study of findability is a fertile area that could expand our understanding of the relationship between DHCs and tools, as well as digital tools' ability to function as viable components of an emerging cyberinfrastructure.

Additional limitations of our evaluation schema became apparent during our analysis of the data. For instance, our evaluation scales favor complex tools that require either uploading of data or downloading of the tool. Simple tools, such as the Web-based Syllabus Finder from GMU, were at a disadvantage in this schema. Though we believe Syllabus Finder to be a very helpful and elegant tool, because it was entirely Web based, it received low downloading and uploading scores. Additionally, it received a low score in clarity of operation, particularly under questions of technical requirements, because there was little need for the sole requirement—a Web browser—to be stated. This particular case suggests that there may be varying models of visibility and usability for Web-based versus downloaded tools. As Web-based applications become increasingly popular, we should reexamine what sorts of documentation and technical specification should be provided.

While our report illustrates a first level of usability for digital humanities tools—access and clarity—we believe there may be an important second level of usability of these tools based upon the field's objectives for tool-based research. A future research question to pursue may be "How well do existing DHC tools respond to the criteria of, and uses for, 'tools'?" As our research questions focused primarily on questions of accessibility and clarity, we excluded tool objectives from our current evaluation of digital tools. We suggest that researchers consider these criteria for further evaluation, as they may provide more insight into the quality of existing tools, and into future development needs in the digital humanities.

Finally, early in the project, we identified questions of institutional support as a valuable factor in defining use and access. This line of inquiry generated additional variables for consideration and additional scales for analyses; however, after careful consideration we felt this particular question would be beyond the scope of the project and perhaps more useful for a follow-up analysis. Appendix F-1 provides the scales and variables associated with this question for possible future use.

7. Bibliography

1. University of Virginia. 2006. *Summit on Digital Tools for the Humanities: Report on Summit Accomplishments*. Charlottesville, VA: University of Virginia.
2. Borgman, C. L. 2007. *Scholarship in the Digital Age: Information, Infrastructure, and the Internet*. Cambridge, MA: MIT Press.
3. American Council of Learned Societies Commission on Cyberinfrastructure for the Humanities and Social Sciences. 2006. *Our Cultural Commonwealth*. American Council of Learned Societies: Washington, DC.
4. Crane, G., A. Babeu, and D. Bamman. 2007. eScience and the Humanities. *International Journal on Digital Libraries* 7:117-122.

8. Appendixes

Appendix F-1:
Tools as Cyberinfrastructure, Institutional Support

We believe a future project could evaluate the 39 tools explored here on a scale that represents the nature of the institutional support for the tool. We will use this scale to provide a descriptive account of the types of institutional support that tools have from DHCs. Describing institutional support for the tool includes:

- a DHC's roles of responsibility for the tool; and
- the level of community collaboration surrounding a tool.

Cyberinfrastructure Scale

Variable	Component	Poor	Moderate	Excellent
Responsibility for tool	Creator Distributor Steward	Creator, distributor and steward are not indicated	One or two of these roles are indicated	Creator, distributor and steward are clearly indicated
Community support for tool	Creatorship Distribution Stewardship	Among jointly authored tools, responsibility for creation, distribution, and stewardship are not indicated	Among jointly authored tools, responsibility for creation, distribution, and stewardship is fuzzy	Among jointly authored tools, responsibility for creation, distribution, and stewardship are clearly indicated

Variable Overview

Variable: Responsibility for Tool	a. Creator-Author		DHC credited as author
	b. Distributor		DHC makes tool available
	c. Steward		DHC is the contact for tool questions, problems
Variable: Community Collaboration on Tool	a. Creatorship	Single DHC	DHC is only organization credited as creator, distributor, or steward
	b. Distribution		
	c. Stewardship	More than one DHC	Collaboration is credited as creator, distributor, or steward
		Outside community	Outside community entity credited as creator, distributor, or steward

Appendix F-2: Scales and Definitions

Questions and Variables	Scales and Definitions				
1a. Word Choice	**Not identified** The broader DHC site does not use a specific term to categorize and identify the item.	**Broader Term** Terms include projects, activities, research, resources.	**Narrower Term** Terms that have a more technological orientation, such as software.	**Tool** Use of the word "tool" to label or categorize an item.	
1b. Visibility	**Not applicable** DHC site does not provide access to a tool.	**Buried** There is no distinct navigation marker to indicate where users can find the tool, but the tool is available on the site.	**List** From the DHC home page, the various resources are grouped and listed together under particular headings, either on side panels of Web page, or within body of home page. This can either be a one-click or two-click link, depending on the construction of the page (i.e., tabs that create separate lists of tools would be a two-click link but a list within body of home page would be a one-click link).	**Featured** A direct link is provided from the first/home DHC page so that users do not have to click to subpages to access the tool or information about it. Typically the name of the tool will be prominently displayed and will not necessarily be categorized within a heading.	
2a. Tool Placement	**Buried** From the DHC home page, the tool can be accessed in more than two links or clicks.	**Two click** From the DHC home page, the tool can be accessed in two links or clicks.	**One click** From the DHC home page, the tool can be accessed in one link or click.		
2b. Downloading - Available	**No** Users are unable to download a version of the tool to use on their personal computers.	**Yes** Users are able to download a version of the tool to use on their personal computers.			
2c. Downloading - Where	**Elsewhere** A link is provided to download the tool from any other type of Web page, aside from the project page and splash page.	**Resources Page** A link is provided to download the tool from a page that lists multiple tools or resources.	**Tool Page** A link to download the tool is provided.		
2d. Uploading - Available	**No** Users unable to contribute their own data to be used with the tool.	**Yes** Users are able to contribute their own data to be used with the tool.			

2e. Uploading - Where	**Elsewhere** Users can contribute their own data to be used with the tool from a page other than the project page or splash page (perhaps when tool is downloaded, people can contribute their data from their own personal computers).	**Resources Page** Users can contribute their own data to be used with the tool from a page that lists multiple tools or resources.	**Tool Page** Users can contribute their own data to be used with the tool from a single site that is dedicated to providing information about the tool.		
3a. Function - Stated	**No** The purpose and intended functionality of the tool are not articulated.	**Yes** The purpose and intended functionality of the tool are articulated.			
3b. Function - Clear	**No** The purpose and intended functionality of the tool are articulated in a such a manner that naïve users cannot understand.	**Yes** The purpose and intended functionality of the tool are articulated in a such a manner that naïve users can understand.			
3c. Function - Concise	**No** The purpose and intended functionality of the tool are described at length or in a roundabout manner.	**Yes** The purpose and intended functionality of the tool are articulated succinctly.			
3d. User group - Stated	**No** The intended audience and tool user group are not articulated.	**Yes** The intended audience and tool user group are articulated.			
3e. User group - Clear	**No** The intended audience and user group are articulated in such a manner that naïve users are unable to identify who will benefit from the tool's use.	**Yes** The intended audience and user group are articulated in such a manner that naïve users are able to identify who will benefit from the tool's use.			
3f. User group - Concise	**No** The intended audience and user group are described at length or in a roundabout manner.	**Yes** The intended audience and user group are articulated succinctly.			

4a. Preview - Available	**No** Site does not provide preview of the tool, where preview is defined as a visible representation of the tool that allows users to get a sense of its look and feel and interaction.	**Yes** Site provides preview of the tool, where preview is defined as a visible representation of the tool that allows users to get a sense of its look and feel and interaction.			
4b. Preview - What type	**Other** Any other representation of the tool that the site provides to give users a sense of the look and feel of and interaction with the tool.	**Screenshots** Site provides a static representation of the tool that gives users a sense of the look and feel of the tool.	**Movies/ Animations** Site provides a dynamic representation of a tool that gives users a sense of the look and feel of the tool.	**Demo** Site provides a sample representation of the tool that allows users to interact with the tool, even if in a limited manner.	**All** Site provides both a screenshot and a demo preview of the tool.
4c. Support provided?	**None**	**Tutorial** Site provides how-to on tool use, such as screenshots accompanied by step-by-step directions or a movie or animation demonstrating tool use.	**Forums** Site provides searchable FAQ or discussion lists about the tool.	**Email** Site provides address for submission of questions by e-mail.	**Live** Site provides a telephone number or another way to solve technical problems with a knowledgeable individual.
4d. Technical Requirements - Stated	**No** Specifications needed to run the software (e.g., memory requirements, OS) are not articulated.	**Yes** Specifications needed to run the software (e.g., memory requirements, OS) are articulated.			
4d. Technical Requirements - Additional Software	**No** Site does not state whether additional software is needed to run the tool.	**Yes** Site states whether additional software is needed to run the tool.			
4e. Technical Requirements - Software Links Provided	**No** If additional software is needed, site does not include links to that software.	**Yes** If additional software is needed, site includes links to that software.			
4f. Technical Requirements - OS	None stated.	Only 1 OS.	Two or more OS.		
4g. Instr. Download - Stated	**No** The site does not include instructions for downloading the tool.	**Yes** The site includes instructions for downloading the tool.			

4h. Instr. Download - Clear	**No** Instructions for download are articulated in such a manner that naïve users are unable to successfully download the tool.	**Yes** Instructions for download are articulated in such a manner that naïve users are able to successfully download the tool.			
4i. Instr. Download - Concise	**No** Instructions for download are described at length or in a roundabout manner.	**Yes** Instructions for download are articulated succinctly.			
4j. Instr. Data - Stated	**No** The site does not include instructions for users to incorporate their own data.	**Yes** The site includes instructions for users to incorporate their own data.			
4k. Instr. Data - Clear	**No** Instructions for users to use their own data are articulated in such a manner that naïve users are unable to successfully use the tool.	**Yes** Instructions for users to use their own data are articulated in such a manner that naïve users are able to successfully use the tool.			
4l. Instr. Data - Concise	**No** Instructions for data use are described at length or in a roundabout manner.	**Yes** Instructions for data use are articulated succinctly.			